FIRM GRIP

FIRM GRIP

Learning To Thrive When Life
Doesn't Go As Planned

BILL NELSON

gatekeeper press
Columbus, Ohio ™

Firm Grip: Learning to Thrive When Life Doesn't Go as Planned

Published by Gatekeeper Press, 2167 Stringtown Rd., Suite 109, Columbus, OH 43123-2839

Printed in the United States of America

ISBN: 9781662914171 (Hardcover)
ISBN: 9781662914188 (Paperback)
ISBN: 9781662914195 (eBook)

Library of Congress Control Number: 2021938812

Editor: Melissa Anne Wuske
Cover Design: Haroula Kontorousi
Interior Design: Davor Dramikanin
Author Image: Lisa Haislet

For all who have walked
through a dark night.

Table of Contents

Introduction:

Losing My Grip

Will I even live to the end of the year?

That was a real question I had after a visit to my doctor. Instantly, my life felt like it was falling apart—worse, maybe ending. In the time it took my doctor to speak a two-word sentence, my life crossed the thin line between comfortable and chaotic. Cast into the balance of life and death. Like flipping a switch—in an instant I saw no light, only darkness.

I have no monopoly on dark days. You've had your share. Maybe you're struggling right now to see through the darkness.

One thing is certain—

the dark finds us all.

If it hasn't found you yet, it will. If it has, it'll come again. From the beginning of time, humans have known suffering, felt its icy embrace, walked a long road as its companion. It's inevitable—none will escape its grasp.

When challenging circumstances cast our lives into the abyss of darkness, everything changes. We feel out of control, and fear takes control. It can be terrifying, crippling even, creating such disruption in our lives that we feel lost, hopeless, and that our best days are now our distant past. Our thoughts turn negative, and we abandon all hope for a better future. We feel like we've lost our grip on life and wonder how we'll get it back—or worse, we fear we'll never get it back.

I know that place. I've lived there, cried there, felt its piercing sting, walked the lonely path of that inner journey, desperate to find a sliver of light to illuminate a way forward. In the pages ahead, I'll share my greatest struggle, and I hope you find your story in mine. I invite you to feel your pain in my pain and face your fears through my fears. I'll be open, honest, and vulnerable, and I'll share how losing my grip—and finding a new one—resulted in discovering a better way of being human. I hope that by the end, you find great hope, and find your new grip.

I suspect you and I are much alike. We've been through some hard days.

But this book really isn't about that.

There's something interesting about our darkest days. Though they arrive like a dangerous storm bent on destroying us, we have an excellent track record for surviving them. In fact, we've survived one hundred percent of the dark days we've faced. It's true. Even though I thought physical death was certain, here I am. I survived. And so did you. Perhaps physical death wasn't what you feared. Maybe you feel like parts of you died from pain, grief, sorrow, and loss. You may feel like pieces of you continue to die each day, chipping away at your soul, slowly stealing any hope to live fully again. Maybe you wonder if life is even worth living after what you've been through.

- But what if you didn't have to live that way?

- What if you could step out of your darkest days and into a bright future?
- What if you could shift the way you think?
- What if you could make new choices that create a positive, hopeful future—no matter what you've suffered?
- What if you could discover a new grip on life that transforms how you live?
- What if you could thrive?

There came a day when I realized I wasn't dying—at least not right now. So, I had to make choices about how I wanted to live for whatever length of time I had left. One option was to be bitter and negative. I'd been through a lot. No one would fault me for asking "why me?" and living in self-pity.

> But I decided living like that
> is just another way of dying.

So, I chose to live positively and hopeful. But to do so, I had to shift the way I think and learn to make new choices—living intentionally, aware of what's happening in and around me, with new ways of engaging my world, new ways of being human. I had to find a new grip on life.

In this book, I'll share my journey through these discoveries. I hope my journey will help you with yours and that you'll realize you have so much more control over your life and future than you imagined. Sure, we might move forward with scars on our skin or heart, maybe even a limp, the imprints of the road we've traveled, but we will move forward. We just have to decide what moving forward looks like. You'll make that choice—so will I.

After our darkest days,
there comes a time we realize
we're not dying.
At least not right now.
Then we have to decide how we'll live.

This
book
is
about
that.

PART I

New Thoughts, New Choices, New Life

01

Your Thoughts Matter

You must learn a new way to think before you can master a new way to be.
—Marianne Williamson

The air in the waiting room smelled stale, as if it stubbornly waited all day for my arrival, pent up and unmoving. The other patients looked at me like they knew something I didn't, like they felt sorry for me. *I'd rather be anyone else in the world right now,* I thought. I checked in at the reception window and was told to take a seat. My wife, Jane, and I chose seats in the corner, far from the door we'd eventually have to walk through to an appointment we didn't want to attend. I couldn't sit still, fidgeting like a seven-year-old boy waiting outside the principal's office.

The waiting room was full of people talking. The conversations all sounded the same, a droning noise with no words. Jane and I sat quietly, unable to speak, or maybe just unwilling. Our thoughts were busy wondering, wandering, and full of uncertainty. I wondered how long before that door opened and someone called my name. Surely it would be a while since all these people were here before me. Certainly,

I had time to pretend everything would be fine or convince myself my research was wrong. I envisioned walking out later, laughing with relief that we had worried for nothing, that I was fine and life would remain our version of normal. A mere moment later that thought was gone, replaced by thoughts I didn't want to think.

Before I was ready, the door opened, and the nurse called my name. I don't remember standing or putting one foot in front of the other, but somehow, I found myself moving through the door. As I entered the hallway, I realized I hadn't smiled at the nurse. *Oh gosh, did I even say hello?* I wondered.

"Third room on the left," she said.

Jane and I made small talk with the nurse as we walked to the exam room, an obvious but lousy attempt to lighten our mood. The nurse said the doctor would be with us shortly as she closed the door, leaving us in the small room. We glanced at each other, knowing the next few minutes might change our lives. Breath was difficult to find, like my lungs were trying to catch oxygen on a cold winter day.

The door opened, too soon again. I wanted a few more minutes in my world where life seemed easy and our problems felt small. The doctor greeted us with a smile, then sat down on his small doctor stool. *Why are those stools so small? Wait… where did that thought come from?* He looked at me, his expression growing more serious. He quickly got to business.

"It's cancer," he said.
It was a two-word sentence
that felt like a thousand punches.

Which leads me to my son Adam and his friend Jake and an early fall evening several years ago.

It was Adam's junior year in high school. Shortly after a family dinner, we couldn't find him. Our house isn't large, so locating him shouldn't have been difficult. But it was. His room was dark. I searched the basement while Jane looked upstairs. He was nowhere to be found. We knew he hadn't left the house, so we called out for him. No answer. I went back to his dark bedroom and turned on the light. There he was, on the floor in a corner, sobbing silently. Something was wrong—really wrong. These weren't the tears of normal teenage troubles.

"What's going on?" I asked.

"Jake died," he said.

"What? What are you talking about?" I asked.

He worked hard to gather himself. His friend Jake collapsed on the high school football field during practice, he told me. Through messages from friends, Adam learned they rushed Jake to the hospital, but he died of heart failure—at seventeen years old.

The hospital overflowed with hundreds of kids, all hoping somehow their presence could bring him back. Jake was one of those kids whose friendships reached far. He wasn't a jock who was just friends with athletes. Jake was friends with everyone. Teachers, coaches, school administrators, parents, and others arrived to help Adam and these kids. But then the kids returned to their homes, wrecked and in irreconcilable pain.

Which leads me to Julie, Jake's mom.

The sudden, unexpected death of her son devastated Julie—that's an understatement. Friends and family can only offer so much support. Julie had to discover ways to deal with her grief, and yet her pain will never fully resolve this side of Heaven. Her life would never be the same.

But her story
wasn't finished.

A Way Forward

How does a person cope with a terrifying diagnosis? How do teenagers deal with the loss of a friend? How can a parent move forward after the he death of a child? These events bring us to a screeching halt, severing our grip on life. Yet these tragedies occur every day, everywhere.

They leave humans in the aftermath looking for a way forward.

But what does moving forward look like? Is life reduced to surviving the days, joyless and miserable, without hope? Is it possible to endure the darkest days of our lives, yet find a way forward into a positive future thriving with hope, joy, and peace? Tragic and catastrophic events present extreme challenges to finding a positive path forward.

Tragedy isn't a required ingredient of a difficult life. Daily life has highs and lows. We all love days that bring joy and excitement. We feel good about ourselves and our lives. We feel alive and hopeful. We think good, positive thoughts. The future looks bright and our lives feel rich and full.

But we also know hard days. They suck the joy out of life. Our thoughts turn negative and our hope is faint. On hard days, negative thoughts often take over. Discontent, we wonder if things will ever improve. If the future looks like the present, we're not interested in taking part anymore.

This book isn't about how to enjoy the good days of your life. The real struggle is dealing with a lifetime that promises to bring many hard days. The emotional ebb and flow of good days and bad days is draining. Feelings of elation turn into feelings of despair, day after day, week after week, month after month, year after year, until we've used up a lifetime.

Have you ever met a person who is negative all the time? They have nothing good to say about anyone or anything. They see no hope for a better future. They have few friends. Life hasn't been fair (according to them). Sadly, we all know people like this.

It's possible
you might be
one of them.

I'm convinced that negative people don't begin life that way. What I believe happened to most of them is at some point they had some rough days—maybe a string of rough days. On those rough days, negative thoughts dominated their minds. They chose to dwell on those negative thoughts day after day and eventually allowed them to take up permanent residence in their head space. Those negative thoughts became a negative focus on life. And that negative focus on life became a way of living.

While most of us probably wouldn't consider ourselves negative people, we've all experienced how too many negative thoughts can impact our lives. Often our negative thoughts come from lies we tell ourselves.

- I'm not good enough.
- I have nothing to offer.
- People like me aren't successful.
- I've made too many mistakes.
- My future is hopeless.

The list is endless. You know your lies—I know mine. The more we tell ourselves these lies, the deeper into a negative mindset we plunge, until we are living negative-focused lives, void of joy or hope.

We don't have to live this way.

We don't have to live in an endless cycle, bouncing back and forth between a positive focus and a negative focus based on our circumstances. I believe that despite difficult circumstances, no matter how bad they are or how frequently they enter our lives, we can consistently live with a sustained positive focus every day. And that is what this book is about.

I have nothing to offer that will prevent difficult times. And I can't share any tricks to eliminate the negative feelings they bring. In fact, just the opposite is true; life guarantees dark days that bring negative feelings of pain, sorrow, and sadness. Feelings are part of what it means to be human. We'll always have feelings, some positive, some negative. But what we'll explore together is an understanding that living a positive-focused life isn't based on our feelings.

Positive-focused living is born from our thoughts.
Today's thoughts become the life we live tomorrow.

Wisdom tradition tells us, "Be careful how you think; your life is shaped by your thoughts" (Proverbs 4:23, GNT) and "For as he thinketh in his heart, so is he" (Proverbs 23:7, KJV). William Channing, a nineteenth century preacher, wrote, "All that a man does outwardly is but the expression and completion of his inward thought."[1] American philosopher, William James, said, "The greatest discovery of my generation is that human beings can alter their lives by altering their attitudes of mind."[2]

We can never live positive-focused lives if our head space is full of negative thoughts. Sure, we can feel sad or scared or lonely. Those are normal emotions we all experience when an undesired circumstance comes. Those emotions are often spontaneous and not of our choosing, and I'm not suggesting they are bad—they are real. But the thoughts we have about those emotions are different.

Our thoughts don't happen on their own.
We create our thoughts.

And our thoughts create our perceptions of reality; they're self-fulfilling. Whether our perception is true or not, it becomes how we live our lives.

Living a positive-focused life doesn't equate with always being happy. Happiness and a positive attitude are not the same. In fact, we can live a positive life even when we aren't happy. Happiness is a feeling that comes and goes, like any other feeling. If you lose your job, you won't be happy. When you get a new job, you'll be happy again. In this book, we'll explore how to choose and maintain a positive focus regardless of your level of happiness.

That could change your life.

Why Listen to Me?

Why would you have any interest in my ideas and opinions about living a positive-focused life? I'll admit that's probably not the best question to ask in the first chapter of a book I want you to read. But it's an honest question. After all, you might have this book in your hands because what you're doing now isn't working for you or at least not in a way that deeply satisfies.

Maybe your life swirls around too much negativity and you feel you're in a tailspin that's draining the joy of living. No matter how hard you try, you can't escape the negative thoughts that occupy the space in your head. Maybe you feel that all you do is survive your days, but long for much more. Or maybe life has dealt you so many bad blows that living a positive-focused life doesn't even seem possible.

So back to my question—what do I offer you?

Let me start by telling you what I don't offer. I don't have degrees in psychology, sociology, or any other discipline that studies the human psyche. I've never conducted studies or experiments on human behavior. I'm not a therapist, life coach, or counselor. I haven't received training in understanding the workings of the human mind.

To be clear, there are many brilliant people who study human behavior. They have the letters after their names to prove it. Their work fills volumes more than this book. And there is much we can learn from them. I'm grateful for people who have dedicated their lives to helping us live ours better. Psychologists, therapists, family counselors, psychiatrists, and life coaches all offer opportunities for us to think more clearly and live more fully. If you need professional help to work through your struggles, get that help. Seek a trained professional who can help you navigate your way back to a fulfilling life.

But I do not have that expertise. Instead, I'm asking you to consider my voice about living a positive-focused life because I'm just a regular guy. Ordinary would be an accurate description.

I'm an attorney living in the Midwest, practicing law for three decades. I'm married to my amazing wife, Jane, and have two adult sons. I have a tribe of people who have helped shape my life and made me a better human. I have over five decades of life experience and have been 'around the block' a few times. Like you, my life has been a cocktail of joy and pain. I've won, and I've lost. I've succeeded, and I've failed. I've had seasons of great clarity and periods when I was unsure of my next step. I've experienced mountain top highs and suffered devastating lows. But at the center of my existence is a deep and sustaining faith in God, integrated and woven into the fabric of my life. It's a faith that transcends religion and breathes life into me.

I've discovered that time and circumstances are among life's greatest teachers. I've learned many lessons, not all of them pleasant or easy. But as I've aged, I've become more aware of these lessons and welcomed their insights. Along the way, one of my greatest learnings has been that our lives will have either a positive or negative narrative.

We filter our lives through one of those narratives.

Positive.

Or negative.

When given the choice—which is every minute of every day—we either choose a negative focus, saturated with negative thoughts which produce negative results, or we choose a positive focus, with positive thoughts that produce positive results. It seems ridiculously obvious, doesn't it? Almost too simple, right? But as simple as the concept is, its truth has earthshaking effects on the quality of our lives because the focus we choose becomes the core of who we are and how we live.

This book explores the pursuit of a positive life narrative through my experiences and commonsense principles and theories you probably already know but may have dismissed because they seem too obvious.

We live in a world where every solution to every problem seems to have a five-step plan for success. I offer no five-step plan. There's no weekend conference to attend or manual to purchase. I will reveal no secrets or shortcuts. I will only remind you of commonsense principles that are obvious and likely already in your arsenal of knowledge.

I could not live out the ideas explored in this book without my faith and belief that there is a Divine plan for my life. And I believe that God's plan for my life is always best, regardless of the fact that it will include difficult circumstances. You see, living a positive life narrative doesn't mean life will always be easy or that positive thinking can chase away the hard times.

Living a positive life narrative
is about intentionally choosing a positive mindset
despite life's difficult circumstances.

You should also know, going in, that I don't have this all figured out. As we'll explore in the next chapter, living a positive life narrative is a daily choice. Often it is a minute-to-minute choice. Choosing to live positive-focused is a lifelong process. Many days, I fail miserably, and my attitude is anything but positive. (Ask my wife. She'll confirm this to be true!) Despite the reality that choosing to live a positive-focused life comes from simple, commonsense principles, it's not an easy task. It takes work and persistent awareness of how we're responding to what is going on in and around us. It takes a moment-to-moment willingness to observe our responses to our circumstances. That's a twenty-four seven job, and it's difficult. But as you explore this book, I hope you conclude that it is worth the effort.

Thought Patterns

I was in my late teens when the television show *L.A. Law* aired. Each week, the lawyers on the show won million-dollar verdicts for their high-profile clients. In their criminal cases, the verdict was always "not guilty." Their clients always had the facts and the law on their side, and everyone was rich. It portrayed the life of a lawyer as a dream profession. Three decades into my law practice, I can tell you that is not the reality of the legal profession.

The practice of law can be a very dark place. Most clients have serious problems—often created from poor choices. They're scared, sad, worried, angry, or bitter—sometimes all of them at the same time. Understandably, they want their attorney to fix their problem. But unlike the lawyers on TV, it's not always possible to fix their problems. Most of the time, all we can do is minimize the consequences.

It's heavy to spend day after day dealing with problem after problem, knowing I can only do so much to help my clients put their lives back together. I've always taken my responsibility to my clients

with utmost seriousness, recognizing they are more than clients—
they are human beings. At times, I've allowed their problems to
become my problems. I've taken thousands of clients' problems home
in my head, to mull over, trying to find the best solution. While that
may be a good thing for my clients, it's not necessarily the best for my
own well-being. It's a fine line between being a zealous advocate for
my clients and maintaining a healthy perspective on my role as their
problem solver.

Many years ago, I made a seismic leap across that line. I'd
witnessed years of carnage in people's lives from poor choices that
resulted in my clients' involvement in the legal system. The results
often had a destructive impact on the lives of my clients and their
families. I struggled to comprehend how so many could make such
destructive decisions. I felt surrounded by this darkness. I became
jaded and cynical, expecting the worst from people. I questioned if
my work was doing anything to bring light to the darkness.

My thoughts became negative and dark and crept into other
areas of my life outside of work. I withdrew from people, even friends.
I felt distant from God. I grew bitter and quiet. Negative thinking
became my default thought pattern. One negative thought led to more
negative thoughts. And the more negative my mind became, the more
negative my life looked and felt. I could fake it when I needed to; but
inside, I became someone I didn't recognize.

This negative life I built lasted far longer than I care to admit. But
I'll never forget the turning point. After once again telling Jane I didn't
care to attend an event with friends, she told me she'd go by herself
as she could no longer live this way. She said even though I appeared
willing to give up our friends, she wasn't. There was something about
that moment, what she said, the way she said it, and the look of pain

in her eyes that gave me a glimpse of my future. And in that future, I was bitter, alone, and miserable.

That turning point started a new journey to reclaim my life. But it wasn't a quick fix. My negative default thinking pattern had become so engrained in my life that it defined who I was, or at least who I was becoming. It took years to break those negative thought patterns and learn new ways of thinking. And it required an enormous amount of intentionality, every moment, to shift the way I thought.

Reflecting on this time in my life, I've come to several conclusions. We choose the thoughts we allow to remain in our head. The thoughts we allow to remain form the basis for more thoughts. Over time, this process develops our default thought patterns. These default patterns become our way of thinking. And ultimately, our default thought patterns shape our view of life. If we develop negative thought patterns, our lives will reflect those negative thoughts. And the opposite is just as true.

Shifting the Way We Think

After Jake's death on the football field, his story made national news. High school football programs around the country offered support to our high school, football team, and community. The Indianapolis Colts even honored Jake. Our community came together, similar to the way our nation came together after 9/11. We were hurting, but we united in our pain and grief. Through this tragedy, we became kinder, gentler, and softer toward one another.

Jake changed us.

Jake's team had an average season that year. With all those kids suffered, no one expected them to accomplish much more than to survive the season. Then something happened as the playoffs approached. The team, rallying around their fallen friend and their season mantra, "Play for Jake," gained momentum in the playoffs, winning game after game. To everyone's surprise, Jake's teammates fought their way to the state championship game. I think we had more residents from our hometown at the game than ones who stayed home.

Despite the scoreboard showing defeat at the final horn, there was nothing but victory surrounding the team and Jake's community that day. His teammates proudly displayed Jake's jersey on the sideline during the game and presented Julie with Jake's runner-up medal after the game.

But then the season ended, and life went on for the players and our community. Somehow Julie had to move forward too, carrying inexplicable pain and grief. Everyone would understand if Julie chose to withdraw from life. No one would judge her for giving up.

But Julie had other plans.

The autopsy revealed that Jake died of an undetected heart condition. A simple medical test could have identified Jake's heart condition and saved his life. Determined to ensure that Jake's life would never be forgotten and his death a catalyst to help others, Julie founded the Play for Jake Foundation (www.playforjake.org), which saves lives by raising awareness of undetected heart conditions in school-age children, preventing sudden cardiac arrest and raising funds so school-aged athletes can get free screenings to check for heart defects. Since the foundation started, thousands of youths have undergone free heart screenings, resulting in the discovery of many previously undetected heart conditions. Each of those kids has received medical treatment for the condition, sparing that child's life and a lifetime of grief for their family.

All of this happened because Julie chose to shift her thoughts. Instead of choosing a thought pattern of negative thinking from a horrible circumstance, she chose to create positive thinking patterns, despite her feelings of pain and grief. Julie chose to create and live a positive-focused life that has a positive, life-saving impact on others. Julie's pain isn't gone. Her decision to shift her thoughts to something positive doesn't eliminate her grief. But Julie's life is proof that living a positive-focused life isn't driven by feelings or emotions; it's about choosing the lens through which you engage the world, no matter what is happening in yours.

Hope

Maybe you've never thought about your thoughts and how they impact your life. They're just thoughts, right? We have thousands of them every day. Most of them come and go. Inevitably, some of these thoughts will be negative. That's normal. And most of our negative thoughts are fleeting. But our thoughts have far more significance in our lives than most of us realize. The thoughts we create inform the narrative of who we believe we are. And the narrative of who we believe we are informs how we interact with the people we engage daily. The thoughts we allow as permanent residents in our minds are particularly powerful.

If you're burdened with negative thought patterns that have created a negative life, I want you to know that you don't have to live like that anymore. Regardless how long you've lived that way, it doesn't have to continue. You aren't doomed nor destined to live a negative life.

- You weren't created to live that way.
- God created you to live with a positive purpose.
- But you have to shift the way you think.
- You have to do the hard work of unlearning thought patterns that robbed you of joy and created a negative life narrative.

> If you don't shift the way you think,
> your past will shape your future.

Romans 12:2 (NIV) says, "Do not conform to the pattern of this world, but be transformed by the renewing of your mind." God is calling you into new ways of thinking, and God calls you to do the work. He doesn't promise there will be no pain or sorrow or tears or that life will be easy. But he promises transformation when you do the renewing work.

If you desire to live the life you were created to live, you have to shift the way you think—there's no other way. Regardless of where you're starting from, this process can't begin without making a choice to change.

So, let's look next at the power of our choices.

02

The Power of Choice

May your choices reflect your hopes, not your fears.
—Nelson Mandela

I don't remember the exact day I met Chuck. I was probably nine or ten years old. But I'm sure we met on a dusty baseball field in our Midwest hometown. Chuck was a couple years older than me. It was the mid-1970s, a time when we rode our bikes to the ball field with our glove hanging on the handlebars, sporting the cap of our favorite team, the Chicago Cubs.

Back then, the days lasted forever. Like time stood still so we could play baseball. We played ball every day all summer. We'd take a break for lunch and then return to finish the game or start another one. When it was time for dinner, my mom rang a cowbell. We could hear it all the way to the field. We went home for dinner, then returned and played until the light faded and we could no longer see the ball.

Those were glorious days.

Chuck could hit the ball a mile. Back then, hitting the ball far was important to me. So, Chuck was someone I admired. He was always one of the team captains. The captains picked their teams with alternating picks. I always hoped Chuck picked me. I never wanted to be a last pick, but if I was a last pick on Chuck's team, that was okay.

Our lives revolved around the game, and so did our friendships. Baseball was our bond. And Chuck was one of my heroes. I wanted to be like Chuck.

As I got older, my friendship with Chuck grew. I liked him for more reasons than just his ability to hit a baseball a mile. A lot of other kids liked Chuck too. He had lots of friends because he was kind to everyone. Even as a kid, I knew Chuck differed from most kids. He was always smiling, always positive. He had a charismatic personality that attracted people.

With age, life took us in different directions. I went to college and Chuck started a construction business. We stayed in touch as much as possible. We both married and had families and ended up living back in our hometown, so we saw each other periodically. We started playing hockey in our thirties and once again, a sport brought us together. And once again, I enjoyed being around Chuck. I felt good when I was with Chuck. I felt better about myself when I was with him. There was still something about him all these years later, the way he treated people, the way he embraced life.

I'll bet there's a Chuck in your life. It was easy for you to identify the Chuck in your life as you read, wasn't it? There aren't many people like them. They're unique—almost one of a kind.

Always smiling.
Always upbeat.
Always positive.

You wonder how they thrive like that, don't you? More so, you wonder how you can thrive like that—or if it's even possible. What is their secret? How are they always so positive? It's as if they've never known suffering. But you know differently. You know they've had struggles. Despite difficulty, they live their lives in an almost magical state of hope.

These folks seem to have something that you are... missing.

It's not that you're never happy. There are many days you feel the positive vibes. Like right after your boss gives you a nice, fat raise. Or when it's five o'clock on Friday, and you've got great weekend plans. Or when you drive home in that shiny new car. Maybe accomplishing a big goal puts you on cloud nine. Who's not in a state of bliss when holding their newborn child for the first time? Or on graduation day? Or when you move into that new house? Or marry your true love?

These moments brought you joy—made you feel that life was worth living—made you feel alive! When moments like these come into your life, it's like a breath of fresh air with renewed hope. You look back on these moments fondly and long for more of them.

And that's the problem, isn't it?
These moments don't *last*.

After a while you increased your monthly expenditures and waited for your next pay raise. That awesome weekend trip ended too soon, and you're back in the office on Monday morning. The shine of that new car faded, and next year's model has better bells and whistles. You accomplished that long sought-after goal only to find it didn't provide lasting satisfaction. After you brought your newborn home, you got three hours of sleep each night and walked around like a zombie during the day (and then they grew up!). The college diploma on your wall faded. Your house needs updating. And your marriage takes effort to maintain.

It's easy to see the pattern here, isn't it? These cool things that come and go in your life are circumstantial. And while these things are a great part of life, none of them provide long-term happiness. What's worse: These circumstances don't come around often.

The temptation is to chase, seek, and create new circumstances that bring happiness, joy, and a positive feeling about your life. You look for your next fix: a bigger house, better job, or new hobby.

On and on it goes to the point of exhaustion and misery, and often it's worse than simply being ineffective at producing happiness: your bad decisions actually deliver the opposite of what you're seeking. You're worn out, depressed, and filled with negative thoughts. Not exactly the positive life you wanted, huh? Not the positive life my friend Chuck lives or that friend of yours you thought of a couple pages back.

You want what they have—something that lasts.

Something that will create a sustained, positive foundation in your life.

Chuck's Choice

Several years ago, I was in my office early on a Monday morning when Chuck's brother called. He told me Chuck was in a motorcycle accident in Virginia. It was bad. Chuck was alive, but he suffered a spinal cord injury. If he lived through surgery, he'd have permanent paralysis from the chest down.

I felt sick.

Not Chuck.

This couldn't happen to Chuck.

My mind raced through decades of friendship with Chuck. So many great memories. So many baseball games played on that dusty ball field. I could picture the big smile that seemed permanently etched on his face. I could hear his larger-than-life laugh. And I could feel his hugs as if he was right there in my office.

That morning I pleaded with God to spare his life.

I'm confident God heard from many of us that day. He survived a delicate surgery, and the doctors put him back together as best they could. But Chuck wouldn't walk out of the hospital. The doctors said Chuck would never walk again.

After the initial recovery, Chuck transferred to a rehabilitation facility in Chicago, much closer to our hometown. I couldn't wait to see him. As I drove to Chicago, I wondered what his life would be like now. Those thoughts were difficult, and I forced them away. It was unbearable to think of a life so vibrant, so positive, so well-lived now forced into a wheelchair.

I had a lump in my throat and was short of breath as I entered Chuck's room. I walked to his bed, leaned down and gave him a hug. And then I lost it. I tried hard to hold back, but this was just too much. I gathered myself and apologized as I knew he needed strong people speaking words of strength to him, not blubbering idiots soaking him with tears.

Chuck looked at me,
and with a trademarked Chuck smile said,
"Brother, I'm gonna be just fine."

Life for Chuck hasn't been easy since his accident. He's had multiple surgeries and suffered many complications. Besides his physical struggles, his daily life changed. He made his living running a successful construction company where he still swung a hammer and worked the jobs. That is gone along with the income and sense of pride a man gets from knowing he's providing for his family. The simple task of getting in and out of a car creates difficulties most of us never consider.

A tragedy in a person's life like this can push them into a physical, emotional and mental downward spiral from which they never recover. After Chuck's accident, I found myself angry, declaring how unfair this was. Chuck was too good a person to have his life torn apart like this.

But Chuck is not your ordinary human—well, he is a human, just like any of us, but he's made extraordinary choices in his thoughts and actions. His spirit is far larger than even I realized. When Chuck said to me, "Brother, I'm gonna be just fine," he wasn't just trying to ease my pain. He proclaimed that this was not how his story would end—that he'd find his grip on life again.

Despite everything he's been through, Chuck has maintained his positive life narrative. I'm confident he's had many dark, private moments where the temptation to give up was great, but his spirit remains positive, day after day, month after month, year after year.

There's something we need to learn from Chuck's life: a positive-focused life isn't a personality trait. Chuck wasn't just born happy and lucky. His outlook was not based on having wealth and big houses or expensive things—we all know some miserable people who have all of that. It's clear that circumstances can't create a positive-focused attitude toward life because our circumstances can change as often as we change our socks. If we allow our feelings to determine our attitude, well, that can create an impressive rollercoaster ride of daily, sometimes hourly, ups and downs.

What's Chuck's secret?
How does he thrive even though his life didn't go as
planned?
It's simple.
It's a choice.

A positive-focused life is simply waking up every day and choosing to be positive that day. That's what Chuck does. Every day, despite his circumstances, despite physical pain, despite the temptation to slip into depression, he makes a simple choice to live that day—just that day—with a positive attitude.

One day at a time.

That's the difference between Chuck and others who dredge through each day, allowing their circumstances to determine their attitude and approach to their day. Seems too simple, doesn't it? Like there should be more. But I already told you there was no five-step plan.

Each day when you wake up,
whether you realize it,
you choose either a positive
or negative focus to your day.

The Power of Choice

- Have you ever considered the extent to which your choices determine the life you live?
- Have you thought about how many choices you make daily?
- Are you aware how often you make choices without even realizing you made a choice?
- Did you know that not making a choice can still be a choice?
- Have you ever considered that the life you live today reflects your past choices?

Having the ability to choose is powerful. Whether we realize it, we exercise that power hundreds, sometimes thousands of times each day. There are very few circumstances that don't present the opportunity to make a choice. And when the opportunity to choose arrives, seldom can we escape the requirement to make a choice. Simple things such as going to a restaurant force us to choose. You choose your meal from options on the menu. But first you had to choose the restaurant—which required that you choose between staying home for dinner or going out. But before that you decided you were hungry, and you wanted to eat. See what I mean? We make choices all the time, not even realizing we are making choices.

But there are some things in life over which we have no choice: Genetics. Skin color. Gender. Our parents. How and where we were raised. Our blood relatives. Our physical characteristics. Hereditary health issues.

We have no voice, no choice in any of these. Handed to us at birth, they serve as our starting point from which we build what we call our life. Looking at this list, some of us feel cheated, others lucky.

Regardless, this is where we start. Pretty much everything else that comes our way presents us with a choice.

Many of our choices are small, inconsequential even. For example, what you wear today, which music you listen to, which show you watch on television. All of them are choices. But they're not likely to have a significant impact on your life.

Other choices have a monumental impact on your life—

Education.

Career.

Geographic location; where you live.

Faith and spirituality.

Marriage.

Children.

Finances.

Values.

Relationships.

The choice to pursue higher education often determines a person's ability to get desired employment at a higher level of income. Alternatively, the choice to skip classes in high school and put little effort into study results in fewer career options and lower earning potential.

Consider how a career choice affects your life. Before I went to law school, I was interested in aviation. I think now how my life and that of my family would have been so much different from the life we've lived. Not bad, just different.

Maybe you dated others before marrying your spouse. How would life be different had you married a different person? Or what about your decision to have or not have children. Can you even imagine your life had you made the opposite choice? Massive changes, right?

Even issues such as finances and how we spend our money have a significant, long-term impact on our lives. A decision to buy the bigger house or luxury car comes with financial consequences that often follow us for years. Whether we invest in a retirement account will impact when and if we can retire.

Our choice of values, the essence of who we are as people, and how we make moral decisions impacts our lives, and how we function in society and interact in relationships. Decisions about faith and spirituality have a massive impact on our worldview, and how we live, interact with others, and process life and all that comes our way. To practice and live a faith-based life is a choice. In what or whom we place our faith is a choice.

Our lives today
reflect the choices we've made in the past,
and the choices we make today
create our future.
It's that simple.
And it's that real.

Eyes Wide Open

I've represented many clients in the criminal justice system. Occasionally, I hear stories from some about their past, how they grew up, the difficulties they faced and the poor decisions they made. Some express regret and remorse about the lives they've lived. Others make dramatic changes and choose to leave the life of crime behind.

They realize the futility in wasting their lives in prison and take steps to finish school and learn skills to re-enter their communities where they can work and become productive citizens. But that is all delayed. Their past choices have earned long-term consequences, in the form of prison sentences to serve before they can begin new lives in society. Their choices shaped their actions, and their actions produced long-term consequences.

Not only do our choices impact our lives, our choices impact the lives of others around us. Just ask the kids of those prisoners how their parent's past choices impact their lives today. Or ask the spouse of an unfaithful partner. Our choices transcend far beyond us into a future that touches many people.

Every day we have the power,
through our choices,
to shape our lives and the lives of those we love.
But one step further—

We have the power to *create* our futures through the
choices we make today.

People like Chuck understand this. They live with their eyes wide open, fully aware of the power of choice. And people like Chuck also understand that living a positive life narrative is nothing more than waking up each day and making a choice to be positive. To find the good in the bad. To push through the ashes to find beauty. To see the joy amidst the pain. To offer love over hate. To see that good will always prevail over evil. To understand that even though life isn't fair, it's always worth living. And to know that every day we are all granted the same twenty-four hours—it's simply a matter of choosing how we live them.

Choosing to Create and Live a Positive Life Narrative

If creating and living a positive life narrative is as simple as choosing a positive mindset, then this book should end now, right? I mean, I haven't told you anything you didn't already know. You weren't likely startled to read that every day you can choose to live with a positive attitude. Just wake up each day and choose to be positive. End of story.

The story doesn't end there because many people live in the struggle of just trying to survive the day because they see no hope for tomorrow. You probably know many people that live that way. Maybe you're one of them. Maybe you see no path to choose a positive focus *on* your life because you see little positive *in* your life. Life's problems seem too deep and feel too heavy. You want to choose a positive focus, but not long after crawling out of bed, your head swirls as you realize yesterday's problems weren't last night's nightmares.

You're overwhelmed and see no way out.

That's why there's more to explore in this book. Let's face it— choosing to create and live a positive life narrative might be as easy as making that choice each morning, but living moment to moment in that choice is hard. Sometimes it's hard to get past nine o'clock in the morning before negativity creeps back in and takes us hostage for yet another day.

You're not alone. This is no easy path, but it's a path we must learn to travel if we'll ever escape the downward spiral of negativity.

And it's not impossible.

For most of my adult life, I've enjoyed the outdoors. I've spent many hours in the woods, walked fields and fence rows, and sat along the shores of ponds and rivers, watching, and learning the habits of various wildlife species. I've concluded that deer are lazy creatures. When given the opportunity, they always take the path of least resistance. If presented the options to walk among the trees or an open cut trail, they'll take the trail. They always choose the easier path.

People are like deer. Most humans choose the path of least resistance. It's natural to want the easy way because it's usually far less messy. But as we learn over time, the easy way isn't always the best way. It's no different with choosing a positive attitude. While most of us don't intentionally choose to live a negative-focused life, when we aren't intentional about choosing a positive mindset, we settle for the easy path which is to respond to life based on the circumstances that come our way. We're positive and upbeat when our circumstances are good, and we take a deep dive into negativity when our circumstances turn ugly.

When we allow our circumstances to control whether we'll have a positive or negative mindset, we give up our power. And when we give up our power, which ironically is a choice, our circumstances dictate our mindset. When that happens, put on your seatbelt because you are in for a long and bumpy ride. Yet, this is how many of us live. That's no way to live, and I want you to know this:

You don't have to live like that!

Some circumstances are self-created as products of good choices we've made. Others feel more like self-inflicted wounds. And other circumstances arrive in our lives that are outside our control. That's life. But even with circumstances outside your control like deaths, illnesses, and other peoples' bad actions...

You have 100 percent control over how you choose to respond.

It's always about a choice. The good news is that you get to make that choice. And with your choice comes great power because when you choose to remain positive despite difficult circumstances, you control your life rather than allowing your circumstance to control your life. Can you imagine how your life would thrive if this was your approach—if you took control over your response to the circumstances of your life? If you chose to remain positive, even in your darkest days?

Abraham Lincoln said, "Most folks are as happy as they make up their minds to be." I've learned that we find what we're looking for in life. Usually, the ugly stuff is easy to spot. But if we look for hope despite despair, we find it. If we look for joy amidst sorrow, it's there, waiting to be discovered. We can choose to be haunted by a difficult past, or we can choose to learn from it and create a better future. But it requires a shift in the way we think and new, intentional choices.

Every minute we choose to be negative is a wasted minute we'll never get back. Life doesn't offer any do-overs. You can choose to be intentional every day and choose to live focusing positively on your life. Fortunately, or unfortunately, it's not a one-time decision. It's a decision you must renew every day.

But you can start any time,
any hour,
any minute.

I don't pretend this is easy. It takes work and effort. It requires a commitment to refusing to waste another minute of your life in negativity. And positive, hopeful people still have lousy days and negative thoughts (just ask Chuck). But positive people choose to let them go.

Take Back Your Power

As you've read up to this point, maybe you've realized you surrendered your power a long time ago. At some point in life, you gave in to the storm of circumstances that ebbs and flows into your daily life, bringing rolling waves. With each high wave that rolls in what you perceive to be something good in your life, you ride that high and feel that life is good and fair. But you ride guarded because as sure as the waves are wet, you know that the low tide will eventually follow and when it does, when life turns on you and something negative flows in, you come crashing down off the wave, and it feels like you hit the bottom of the ocean floor. With the crash comes feelings of despair, loss of hope and emptiness.

If you're tired and worn out from the ride, this book is an invitation to take back your power—to decide you'll live differently—to choose a positive focus even amidst trials, challenges, and dark circumstances.

I'm far from perfecting this in my life. Every day I wake up and have to choose to go out into my world with a positive mindset. It does not come naturally, and it does not always come easy. I've lived far more days with a negative focus than I care to admit. And then, I changed my life by choosing to live differently.

You can join me in that decision by choosing to take back your power. That doesn't mean we celebrate and throw a party when life dumps on us. And it doesn't mean we'll avoid anger, sorrow, pain, and the other emotions that accompany difficult circumstances. There is no level of positive thinking or living that will fix every problem or spare us from heartbreak. Choosing to live with a positive mindset means we don't dwell in those negative emotions. Positive-focused living means that we choose to find hope despite our problems and difficulties.

> The future won't be better by accident,
> it will only be better by choice.
> Intentional choice.

But…

I know what some of you are thinking—this guy doesn't understand how bad my life is. He has no idea how many poor choices I've already made. He has no clue how terrible my circumstances are. He doesn't understand the depth of my pain. He doesn't know how hopeless my situation is. You're right. I don't know the circumstances of your life. I recognize that choosing to create and live a positive life narrative when life seems so dark can make that choice feel impossible. But I can also tell you that darkness eventually finds us all.

It's inevitable because every day has its night.

03

Every Day Has its Night

The darkest hour has only sixty minutes.
—Morris Mandel

Forty-three years. That's how long I lived before real darkness crashed into my life. That's a long time to live without experiencing deep pain or suffering a significant loss. People actually teased me about it. I was told many times I'd never known what hard times really were, that I'd been born under a lucky star, that my life had been way too easy to understand the true struggle of life. There was probably some truth in that. Sure, I'd had some days that weren't so bright, but who doesn't, right? I'd seen a cloud or two, even some threatening storms. But those clouds never fully developed into storms that brought serious chaos into my life. Oddly, I was aware of how many bullets I'd dodged and the rarity of living that long without experiencing personal tragedy or loss.

But I knew life wouldn't stay that way.

Just days after my forty-third birthday, I sat at a middle school basketball game watching my son Erik play in a tournament. It was a Saturday morning in the dead of winter. My phone rang. On the other end was a friend who was a local physician. He said, "Bill, if you want to see your father before he passes, you better get to the hospital quickly."

Fourteen years prior, my father began a long road with heart disease. He'd had, on average, one medical procedure per year during that fourteen-year stretch to keep him alive. His run with heart problems started when my younger son Adam was an infant. We were grateful modern medicine extended my father's life and gave my sons an opportunity to know their grandfather.

When I arrived at the hospital, I found my mother gathered with some family friends. Soon after, the doctor came out to inform us my father died. I didn't get to say goodbye or tell him I loved him.

But I *know* he knew.

Those words from the doctor marked the first time real darkness found my life. I felt a deep pain, the likes of which I'd never experienced. I lost other loved ones and family friends over the years, but none of that pain felt like this. This was my father. I was his only son. We had that unique father-son connection that now felt eerily distant. I knew I had just entered a different realm of life, the realm of deep pain, sorrow, and anguish.

The dark eventually finds us all. Hard days, difficult struggles, and deep pain will come. It's inevitable. I often say, "If you haven't experienced dark days, you simply haven't lived long enough." None of us escape this life without experiencing pain, often physical, but almost always emotional. It's like a rite of passage, but a rite we'd prefer to pass us by. But it isn't possible. The darkness comes and forces us to face it, endure it, survive it somehow, someway. Even once the darkness has passed, deep pain leaves its mark, like a permanent tattoo. We carry that pain. And often, that pain becomes a weight that drags us down under its burden.

As life throws more difficulty our way, our burdens multiply and grow heavier, even unbearable. We can experience so much pain and anguish we begin to believe life will never improve, that we're destined to live without joy or hope for our future. Our minds dwell on our pain, the thoughts we create turn dark, the choices we make birth despair, and we end up living a negative-focused life. We don't wake up one day and choose this path. But over time our negative thought patterns inform our choices, our choices shape our lives and the outcome is living with a negative focus.

You're probably no stranger to this struggle. Most likely you've already met sorrow. You've held the hand of pain. You've walked alongside despair. Your load is heavy, your will is weak and you're close to losing your grip. Maybe you already have. Maybe you've already decided this is just the way your life will be—dark. As a result, your mind space is full of negative thoughts and you have little room for even the idea of hope.

The death of a loved one, a financial crisis, serious medical issues, a betrayal—these issues are real, and these issues cause deep wounds and pain. I'll never pretend that choosing to create and live a positive-focused life will fix these troubles. But you still have a choice in how you respond to them. When the dark stuff comes, we either choose the path of anger, fear, bitterness, and self-pity, or we choose a path of hope.

My Dark

It was the fall of 2015. I was driving to work when I heard what sounded like a blown speaker in my car. The music sounded distorted with a crackling noise. The distortion was most noticeable in my right ear. The noise drove me nuts—so much so I had to turn the radio off and drive in silence. It continued all week. On Friday, I stopped at a friend's auto shop and asked him to listen, to help me figure it out so we could fix it. He didn't hear the crackling sound. That was crazy—the distortion was obvious. Apparently, he had a hearing problem, I reconciled. The next day I was with my wife, driving her car. Turning her radio on, the reality of the situation became clear—her speaker sounded cracked too.

The problem was me—my hearing.

About a decade prior, I had a serious issue with my left ear that required surgery. The surgery failed, creating substantial hearing loss in that ear, and left me wearing a hearing aid. So, my right ear was my good ear. I needed that ear at full strength. How good can an attorney be in a courtroom if he can't hear?

Over the next several weeks, the distorted hearing came and went. Oddly, it was only noticeable in a car, probably some small cabin acoustics thing, I rationalized. I figured I just had a sinus infection and let it go, turning off the radio on the bad days.

Later that fall, I had a dizzy spell. Nothing too serious. I could function normally, and it resolved in about ninety minutes. I mentioned it to my wife, but neither of us gave it much thought until it happened again a couple weeks later while I drove to work. Again, nothing terrible. I was able to continue driving, and an hour or so later it ended. This time my wife insisted I call an ear, nose and throat specialist (ENT). I reluctantly agreed, protesting it was just a stubborn sinus infection.

The appointment with the ENT led to a visit with my audiologist which led to a referral to another ENT, this one an expert in diagnosing unusual hearing disorders. While waiting for that appointment a few weeks later, the distorted hearing seemed better, and I had no more dizzy spells. I intended to cancel the ENT appointment, but my wife objected. To appease her, I agreed to go, so she'd see everything was fine and I was correct in my self-diagnosis of a lingering sinus infection. As if Divinely urged to avoid a last-minute cancellation, the morning of the appointment, I had a serious dizzy spell, one that almost caused me to fall.

While explaining my hearing history to the ENT and the bizarre events of the past couple months, he performed a full ENT exam. With his fingers pressed firmly into my throat, he asked if I knew I had a thyroid nodule. I said no and asked what that meant. (Full disclosure: I have to admit I was vaguely aware our bodies had a thyroid. But I wasn't sure of its exact location, nor had any clue how the thyroid functioned or what it did for the human body). His response informed me the nodule was likely nothing and approximately eighty percent of adults have thyroid nodules, the vast majority of which are benign. The word benign was a bit unsettling as I knew the opposite of benign was not a good thing when talking about lumps and bumps in the body. He said we'd check it out, then immediately returned his questions to my hearing problem and dizzy spells.

At this stage of the appointment, I was no longer thinking much about a likely sinus infection. I wanted to know what this nodule was in my neck. My mind was on lumps and bumps when the doctor said he wanted a computed tomography scan (CT) of my head so he could look for inner ear abnormalities. He handed me a written order for the CT and told to come back for the results in a couple weeks.

"What about the nodule?" I asked.

"Oh yeah," he said, almost as an afterthought, then handed me another order for an ultrasound of my neck. His carefree attitude about the nodule relaxed me. If he could forget about it so quickly, so should I.

A couple weeks later, I had the CT and ultrasound tests, then left to spend the holidays in Florida with my family. To my delight, the symptoms stopped completely. The hearing distortion ended, and I suffered no further dizzy spells after the big one the morning of the appointment.

After a relaxing trip, I returned to the ENT to get my test results. I had no concerns about the CT due to my renewed confidence it was just a sinus infection that had resolved. The ultrasound results of my neck were of greater concern to me. Although there was a mysterious lump in my thyroid, it caused no pain and I could barely feel it. It too was likely nothing and life would go on as normal, I reasoned. But my concern lingered.

The CT results weren't back yet, but the ultrasound report was. Although my doctor provided no details from the report, he said he wanted a biopsy of the nodule to rule out any serious possibilities. Asking if it worried him, he quickly reassured it was just precautionary, and he had no serious concerns. His words, and particularly his delivery, were reassuring so neither I nor Jane left with any real apprehension.

Just a biopsy.
No big deal.

Another couple of weeks passed, and I found myself on a table, the surgical pathologist apologizing for what he's about to do. He told me I would feel no pain (the meds took care of that), but I would feel enormous pressure on my neck.

"How much pressure," I asked.

"Like I'm standing on your throat," he said.

And that's exactly how it felt. When he completed the biopsy, I sighed my relief—until he told me he needed two more samples. By the time I got home, the swelling looked like I had a tennis ball in my neck.

I had an appointment scheduled to see the ENT ten days later for the results. Two days after the biopsy, my doctor's office called. The friendly lady on the phone said my doctor wanted to move the appointment up to my first availability. I knew that wasn't good. I scheduled for two days later, hung up the phone, and said out loud to myself…

"I have cancer."

Lawyers thrive on facts. Having all the facts can make or break a case in court. Not having all the facts can lead to disastrous results. I don't act without all the facts, and I wouldn't start now. I turned to my computer where Dr. Google informed me there are four varieties of thyroid cancer. Who knew? One and two on the list are very common, account for about ninety percent or more of all thyroid cancers and are both highly curable. That was a good start to this research project.

Number one on the list accounts for eighty percent of all thyroid cancers. It's called papillary thyroid cancer.

The worldwide web also informed me that thyroid cancer types three and four on the list are extremely rare and incurable, accounting for the most thyroid cancer deaths. My mind thinks logically, lineally and based on known facts, trained that way in law school and honed over years of practicing law. That trained mind quickly determined the high likelihood I had the first type on the list—papillary thyroid cancer.

Over the next couple days, I learned all I could about papillary thyroid cancer so I could engage an intelligent conversation with my doctor. Feeling informed, I had all my questions ready and was confident about the appointment. To someone who thinks the way I do, knowledge is power. In the strangest way, I felt in control. I'd done my homework and was confident of what was ahead.

Deeper Shades of Dark

On the way to the doctor appointment, my confidence was more rattled than I expected. Jane and I didn't talk much in the car. I was about to be told I have cancer. Let's face it—that sucks, even when you know it's coming.

After the awkward greeting and handshake, my doctor turned stoic.

"It's cancer," he said, with an obvious look of concern.

"Papillary?" I asked.

"No, medullary," his expression now more serious.

I knew three things in that moment:

1. Medullary thyroid cancer was one of the types I *really* did not want to have.
2. Medullary thyroid cancer is rare, incurable, and deadly.
3. I knew little about medullary thyroid cancer and wasn't prepared for this conversation.

Heart pounding, head spinning, sweaty palmed I asked, "Is this going to kill me?"

With a less than confident look and a slight turn of his head, my doctor said,

"Probably not."

While that response should have provided comfort, I believed this guy was too kind and compassionate to tell me anything else in that moment, even if he knew I would drop dead the next day. My wife asked what the next steps were, and he said he was referring me to a surgeon at a large university hospital who specialized in the extensive surgery I would need.

The drive home was surreal. It's one thing to be told you have cancer. I expected that. It's an entirely different game to be told your cancer is rare and incurable. I was quiet. I didn't know what to say or think.

There was no emotion at all.

I felt nothing.

Shortly after arriving home, and completely against Jane's advice, I consulted Dr. Google again. If there was ever a time I should have listened to my wife, it was then. Less than ten minutes into my search, it was clear (in my mind) I was dying—and fairly soon.

I was no longer numb.
I was no longer without emotion.
Fear set in and took control.
My emotions erupted and I lost my grip.

It's interesting, sad even, how I almost feel shame when writing those words. It's as if I think I should have been man enough and tough enough to have felt no fear nor shown any emotion. If I had a stronger faith in God, I try to convince myself, I should have been brave and courageous in those moments, instead of turning into an emotional wreck.

But I'm reminded of Jesus in the garden the evening before his death. Fully God, yet also fully human, Jesus prayed, cried out even, asking his Father to "remove this cup from me." As God, he knew what lied ahead, but in his humanness, he was mindful of the agony he would suffer. We're told he sweat drops of blood, which is a biological result of extreme stress when capillaries break and blood mixes with and seeps out through sweat. There is great peace in knowing the Divine understood exactly what I experienced that evening. Feeling fear and expressing emotion are simply part of the human experience. That night my human experience was raw and intense and never more real.

Despite her best efforts, Jane couldn't console me. So, she left. She got in her car and left. I was thinking the same thing you're thinking right now—how could she? But my wife is wise. She knew what I needed. She left to find our closest friends and brought them back. We spent the evening with our dear friends, Mark and Lesa. Mark and I go back to age eight; he's like a brother in so many ways. We cried together, got strong together, then fell apart again together. But we were together.

The next morning, I awoke (if waking can even happen after a sleepless night) to my new reality. I had an incurable cancer. I knew little about it, had no idea what the future held and didn't even know what next steps looked like, other than I was going to Indiana University Medical Center to see a new doctor—a doctor I hoped would figure out a way to save my life.

It was a Saturday morning, and I knew I had to do what I did every Saturday morning: go to the gym. At the gym, I felt like I had a secret nobody else knew. The other people knew me, but they had no clue what I was going through that day.

There I found my first bit of strength amidst the chaos. I was sitting on a weight bench, looking in the mirror. I looked healthy. I was fit and lean. I looked anything but sick. I felt fine. I was strong and full of energy.

How could this person I saw in the mirror have an incurable cancer that could end his life? I thought to myself.

In that moment I felt overwhelmed with a sense of survival, a strong sense of determination this would not be my end, a deep belief that day was the start of a new journey that was calling out, challenging me even, asking if I was up for the task.

Resolve replaced fear.

For the moment…

Over the next few weeks, I learned the most difficult aspect of this type of darkness: the unknown. I had so many questions, yet so few answers. For an attorney who thrives on details, not knowing was more difficult than even bad answers. I returned to my research to learn about medullary thyroid cancer (MTC). That did not include Dr. Google this time. Instead, I read the medical guidelines that are the standard for treatment of MTC. With knowledge came many answers and more questions. Knowledge brought peace, but also created more opportunity for the return of fear. This much was clear: MTC is a deadly cancer; traditional forms of radiation and chemotherapy are ineffective on MTC; the only real treatment was surgery.

One option.
One hope.

Ear to Ear

I met with my new doctor in Indianapolis—Dr. Avinash Mantravadi, a young rock star surgeon. He ran tests to determine if the cancer had metastasized to my lungs, liver or the lymph nodes in my neck, areas where MTC frequently spreads. Our first good news was that my scans detected no metastasis—very good news. But the blood tests showed high numbers for MTCs two tumor markers, creating concern the scans may have missed metastasized MTC. Fear once again knocked at the door, wanting in, desiring to consume my spirit.

The battle within was constant—
and exhausting.

My tumor board, a medical panel comprising eight physicians of varying disciplines, scheduled my surgery. It was reassuring to know many brilliant minds were collaborating on the best approach to my medical care. It was also a reminder how serious my situation was that it required that many brilliant minds for one patient.

I continued to work, trained at the gym, and carried on my normal life as much as possible while waiting for surgery. People told me I was brave, the way I was handling it. But honestly, I didn't feel brave. I didn't have any choice. The sun kept rising every day so, so did I. Jane and I decided to make my diagnosis public. We live in a smallish community and knew it would be difficult to keep the information secret for long. We also believed if we controlled the release of information, we could make sure the truth got out. But most importantly, we desired the support and prayers of our many friends in our community—we received it and are forever grateful.

The three-hour drive to Indianapolis the day before my surgery felt like six hours. But Jane and I have close friends who refused to let us take this journey alone. Mark, Lesa, Rob, Rod and Miki joined us in Indianapolis the night before surgery. We went to dinner, told stories, laughed and did everything we could to distract ourselves from the events of the next day. These amazing friends were at the hospital ridiculously early the next morning to greet us upon our arrival. It's a Divine moment when the people who love you pray over you as your name is called for surgery. Later that morning, our dear friends Gerry and Roxy also arrived to support Jane during the surgery.

Surgery lasted eight hours, the initial recovery another three. The surgeon removed my thyroid along with just about everything in my neck that I didn't need to live or keep my head attached. I came out of surgery with a twelve-inch, ear-to-ear incision.

Guided by the hand of God, my doctor performed the surgery flawlessly, dodging the long, terrifying list of possible complications he'd told me about. All indications pointed to a successful surgery.

Yet my surgeon, as skilled as he is, couldn't tell me it was all over, that everything would be fine, and there was no more cancer. Only time would reveal my prognosis. I spent the next two days in the hospital, before being released for the long ride home.

My sons came home from college to spend time with me upon my return. We were all together when my surgeon called late in the evening to check on me and tell us the results of the post-surgery pathology report. Forty-two lymph nodes were removed from my neck. All but two were cancer-free. I was thrilled with that result, assuming it was a ratio game. Only five percent of my lymph nodes were diseased.

Unfortunately, MTC doesn't follow the rules of ratios, my doctor told me. It's a unique all-or-nothing type of cancer. It spreads early and microscopically. It's important to get the tumor out before MTC leaves the tumor and infiltrates surrounding lymph nodes. The reality was that MTC had escaped the main tumor and likely had freedom to roam my body.

We had to wait ninety days for blood draws to measure the tumor markers that identify the cancer activity in my body. Ninety more days of waiting for some of the most important answers in my life. These answers would determine how far back my surgeon set my clock.

More waiting, more opportunity for fear to take control.

The Space in Between

What does a person do during the ninety-day wait for the results of medical tests that will determine if their life might soon end? How does a spouse survive the days after being told the marriage is over? How does a parent handle having a child addicted to drugs, not knowing what the next phone call might bring?

When the dark ravages our lives, there's a sudden and dramatic attack on our confidence and perceptions of stability. We've become comfortable with our predictable lives and feel in control. We know what to expect and assume tomorrow will look like today.

Yesterday's familiarity suddenly seems a distant past, today feels terrifyingly new and uncomfortable, and tomorrow's unpredictability is overwhelming. We are in a liminal space between known and new. Liminal spaces are fragile, thin spaces where we teeter on an ever so narrow edge, not knowing which way we might fall or what we'll land on. Humans aren't good with liminal spaces. We don't like unpredictability. With the arrival of the dark, often comes the departure of predictability. It's even more difficult to remain in these liminal spaces for lengthy periods of time, waiting for the unknown to become known.

My cancer diagnosis cast me into the space in between. My comfort of yesterday and perceived security of today disappeared. No longer could I assume tomorrow would arrive as I'd planned. I had no idea what my new tomorrow would look like, or even if I had many tomorrows left. Even worse, it would be months before I'd have any answers that might help define my new future. My past no longer felt relevant, yet my circumstance didn't permit me to live in a future tense. I was forced to live in the present moment which now was just a space in between.

And wait.

But there's something interesting about liminal spaces, something that can be beautiful if we have eyes to see. The space in between is where transformation takes place. When our world is shaken to its core by the darkness, we have an opportunity to re-evaluate our lives, to view our lives from new perspectives, to see with new eyes. But we have to be open to allow this process to take place. It can never occur if we let fear, anger, hate, bitterness, despair or other negative emotions take control.

When we let fear, anger, or despair control us,
we've *made the choice* to let it control us.

When the dark arrives, emotions erupt. The dark is scary stuff. It's normal to feel fear. It's normal to feel anger. It's normal to feel pain and heartache and many other emotions. It's part of being human. I'm not telling you to ignore your emotions or that those emotions aren't real. They are very real, and they lead us to lament.

Lament is an indispensable part of living in the space in between. I'm convinced God gave us the space in between so we can experience the gift of lament. Lament is healthy. Lament is sacred. Lament leads to healing. Lament grants freedom to grieve, to mourn, to hurt, cry, scream and even to sit silent, being fully human, feeling all the feelings, as they too are gifts. Lament is a gateway that leads us to more, something better. Lament will almost always bring us full-circle, back to hope.

But it may take a long time—
a very long time.

So let me be clear—
It's okay to be not okay,
we just can't permanently live there.

As we discussed in the first chapter, how we think forms thought patterns that shape our life narrative. But when we decide that painful emotions don't get to stay and take up permanent residence in our lives, we create space to see beyond our pain, live past our fears, and allow for transformation by the journey that lies ahead. That transformation, although difficult, will almost always change us in beautiful ways.

Every Night Has a Dawn

Ninety days after surgery, it was finally time for blood tests to check the tumor markers. Ninety days is the estimated time required for the blood to flush the byproducts of the cancer removed during surgery. These test results would shed light on my prognosis.

Jane and I spent two days in Indianapolis for this testing process—one day for blood draws, the next for the doctor appointment to receive the results. We did our best to distract ourselves during the downtime, yet the weight of the looming results was heavy. When we finally met with the doctor, we learned that one test result was in and had returned to normal range, but the other test result was not yet available. We had half the needed information, and it was good. But we had no option but to leave Indianapolis and await the other test results by phone—more waiting in the space in between. Later that night the call came. My tumor marker was undetectable, the best news possible for this incurable cancer!

Five years later, I'm doing well. I'll have periodic medical tests and blood draws for the rest of my life to monitor this cancer. We know there is a significant possibility the evil remains in my body because of the diseased lymph nodes found during surgery. That's just my reality. But I feel great and live a normal and full life. Will that change? Only time will tell. I'll continue to trust God with my future and my life.

I'm often asked if my cancer is gone and if my battle is over. When I say we really don't know if things will get ugly again, the next question is often, "How do you live with that uncertainty?" I always respond the same—I ask how they live with their uncertainty. That is the reality, isn't it? None of us have any guarantees in our lives, do we? But we know that dark and difficult times will find us all. We have no choice in that reality. But we always have a choice in how we respond to the dark when it arrives.

There's a Light in the Dark if We Choose to See It

It's easy to feel that our lives are falling apart when we go through painful, scary, and difficult times. In the middle of the pain, it's hard to see that God is still at work in our lives. Sometimes the pain is so great, that's all we can see. Yet we can be wrecked, and come out the other side stronger. We can be completely broken, yet made whole.

Not every dark night comes to destroy our lives. Some dark nights come as a guide that eventually lead to a rescued, renewed, and beautiful life that waits on the other side of our pain.

Dark and difficult times will change us—that is certain. If we allow them, they will break us. Or we can choose to rise out of our suffering and open ourselves to what God wants to do in our lives. Traveling through the dark often results in new strengths, fresh perspectives, new resolve and deepened desire to create a new future that leans toward hope:

We've seen the dark,
we lived the dark,
and it pointed us to light.

If given the opportunity to re-write my life, I wouldn't change a thing—not even my diagnosis. It's brought many unexpected and wonderful gifts into my life. It's been the path through which God reshaped my faith once again. It changed my perspectives and created the opportunity to see more clearly the life I'm created to live. My life is different now. Better? No doubt. Uncertain? Absolutely. But it never was certain. I now live with new eyes, new perspectives, and a full heart. I now live each moment fully aware and fully awake.

That's the choice I've made.

I don't believe the words "How did that happen?" have ever come from the mouth of God. He's never caught off guard. He's never blindsided. Not once was he surprised by the events that transpired. My life, the good and the bad, the beautiful and the ugly, the joy and the pain, the laughter and the tears, and even MTC are all part of God's twisting, turning, messy, crazy but perfectly designed plan for my life. Each day, moment, event, smile, tear, breath, and diagnosis have played a role in making me who I am today. Even though I don't always understand his plan, I choose to embrace it because I trust him with all I have and all I am.

As Louie Giglio, a favorite author, wrote, "God is always painting on this canvas that's bigger than we can see or imagine."[1] So, I will walk this beautiful and crooked path, knowing it's my path and for me it is perfect.

04

When God's in Your Boat

To one who has faith, no explanation is necessary. To one
without faith, no explanation is possible.
—Thomas Aquinas

There's a small Eastern Orthodox church in my community. Many years ago, its clergy discovered that a one-hundred-year-old icon in the church was emitting an oily substance from the wounds in the hands, feet, head, and side of the body of Christ depicted in the icon. The clergy announced that the substance was myrrh. For several weeks, the substance flowed. Passionate Christ followers came from all around the nation to observe this icon, creating a traffic nightmare. This church is within a few miles of my house. I drove past it often, frustrated by the traffic jams. But I never went in to see the icon.

Then the flow stopped, and it was over.

Other churches around the world have reported similar events, sometimes occurring in a statue rather than an icon. Sometimes these occurrences make the evening news or show up in our social media feeds. But if you're like me, you drive by, pay little attention or scroll past it on your newsfeed.

Why do most of us care so little about events like these? Is it because we presume it's a hoax? Do we have so little faith in today's clergy that we assume they've somehow rigged the icon or statue to appear to be a modern-day miracle? Maybe some of us never believed in miracles to begin with so we dismiss these events as anything but Divine. I suspect all these reasons may come into play, but I also suspect there is a deeper issue at the core of our disbelief.

I think most people don't believe God interacts in our lives physically anymore, that God is somewhere "out there," but does not interact here, now, in a tangible way. I understand that logic. After all, when was the last time you've seen water turned to wine? When has God ever led you with a pillar of cloud by day or pillar of fire by night, the way he led the Israelites out of Egypt? When was the last time God parted the water in front of you so you could walk across on dry land?

I was raised in a Christian home, and we attended church every week, sometimes multiple times per week. I've heard all the stories of the Bible more times than I can count, many times as a child with flannelgraph boards to help depict how Noah placed two of every animal on the ark. The stories seem miraculous and create great awe about how God acted in the lives of the people in the stories. And I've always believed them, at least in my heart, anyway. But at some deep, subconscious, intellectual level, I have to admit I've struggled a bit to believe the stories, even if I wasn't aware of my struggle. After all, I haven't witnessed miraculous events like these continue in modern-day life.

Despite this confession, I'll also tell you my core faith has never wavered, and I believe God is real and Jesus is his Son who died, rose from the grave, conquered death—and I believe that event changed everything for all time.

But back to the question—why doesn't God interact in our lives the same way today?

Or does he?

You may think I'm crazy after reading what I'm about to say.

I'm okay with that.

In the last chapter about the events I experienced leading up to my cancer diagnosis, I described the sound of crackling speakers in my car and dizzy spells. The noise came and went for about three months. The dizzy spells, although less frequent, happened over the course of those same three months, all culminating in my doctor discovering the lump in my neck on the afternoon of a day when I had my worst dizzy spell and heard the awful crackling noise.

And then both ended.

After the appointment when my doctor found the lump, I experienced no more dizzy spells and the sound of crackling speakers never returned.

Not once.

Ever.

After hearing the diagnosis, Jane asked the doctor about the symptoms and how they related to the cancer diagnosis. To our surprise, he said there was no connection at all—the dizzy spells and distorted music had nothing to do with MTC. Jane then asked the doctor what he thought caused those symptoms. He said there was no medical explanation. Despite our shock from the diagnosis, Jane and I glanced at each other, managed a slight smile, and Jane told him we knew what caused it.

"We call that God," my wife proclaimed.

Those symptoms disappeared on their own,
never diagnosed,
never treated,
and never returned.

Have you ever had a situation in your life you didn't know how to handle? You know, one of those difficult circumstances where you asked God for direction because you didn't know what to do? You looked for the right answer and wished God would speak to you out loud and tell you what to do—because we all know how much easier life would be if...

God would just speak up
and tell us.
Right?

We are convinced God used that series of events to get me to the doctor. To this day, my wife and I believe I heard the voice of God—that God spoke to me. It wasn't in English. It wasn't even a sound that made sense. We believe God spoke to me, and his voice was the sound of cracked stereo speakers.

What was once an irritating noise
became one of the most beautiful sounds
I will ever hear in my life.

I don't know that God will ever part a river for me to cross on dry land, but I'm confident God intervened in and acted within my life physically for his purpose and plan for my life. I believe God spoke in a way that got my attention and got me to the doctor, which resulted in the discovery of my cancer, a discovery that saved my life, or at least prolonged it.

I can't promise you God will act in your life in such a way that you'll know it was him. But I can promise you God will act in your life. No matter what it is you've suffered or are going through now, God has a plan and purpose for your life you can trust. But when the darkness hits hard, fear can set in and words like "just trust God" are seldom enough. So many kind and good-hearted people offered many words of encouragement to me and pointed me to God. But I had to find my path of trust, my way toward a belief that God was in the midst of a cancer diagnosis. That path came, in part, from a gift from friends.

A Pocket Full of Hope

I'm confident that being told you have a rare and incurable form of cancer would have a dramatic impact on anyone. I've no shame in admitting I was terrified. I was 51 years old and wasn't ready to end my time on Earth. I struggled with the fear. Some days were worse than others. Yet I desperately desired to find courage in my faith, a lasting courage that would sustain and bring peace.

After my diagnosis, but before all the medical testing and appointments began, our friends Gerry and Roxy gave me a small packet of cards tied together with a ribbon. The top card read, "Take Courage - A collection of verses and prayers for difficult times."

After times on her own personal dark path, Roxy put this collection together to encourage others. The cards were small enough to carry in my pocket. I took them everywhere—work, the store, out to dinner, you name it, I had them in my pocket.

The verses on the cards reminded me that God loved me and would never leave me. Ever. Whenever I felt fear creeping its way into my mind, I pulled out the cards and read of God's presence and love. The verses reminded me God wasn't one bit worried about nor fearful of my diagnosis. He wasn't wringing his hands in concern or fretting over whether I would survive. He knew of this day before time began. There was peace in knowing the Creator of the universe was on top of this. But there was one verse in particular that was so meaningful and became my go-to verse during those darkest days.

"Don't panic. I'm with you. There's no need to fear for I'm
your God.
I'll give you strength. I'll help you. I'll hold you steady,
keep a firm grip on you."
Isaiah 41:10 (The Message)

This verse helped me find my center. More importantly, it grounded me in my faith. It gave me a source of truth from which fear no longer made sense. This verse didn't remove fear, but provided the means to filter my fear. When fear taunted, demanded my attention, I'd reach into my pocket, clutch those cards in my hand, knowing the truth of the words, and fear fled, replaced by peace and calm, knowing that God held me in his firm grip.

These courage cards accompanied me to every doctor appointment, scan, blood test, and even my surgery, right up to the point they wheeled me to the operating room. Where I went, the truth of these words followed. God's promise to never leave nor forsake us became very real in my life. His love replaced my worries. His firm grip on my life replaced my fear. I can boldly face whatever may come my way knowing his firm grip has never left me.

And it never will.
Ever.

There was a particular moment during these days that reshaped my faith and forever changed my connection to God. But first, I need to tell you about one of my favorite stories from the Bible.

Wind, Waves, and Words

It's a story that includes fear, worry, uncertainty, chaos, stress, anger, shock, awe, intrigue, surprise, and even the threat of death. It's an intense story of epic proportion suitable for the big screen.

"That day when evening came, he said to his disciples, "Let us go over to the other side." Leaving the crowd behind, they took him along, just as he was, in the boat. There were also other boats with him. A furious squall came up, and the waves broke over the boat, so that it was nearly swamped. Jesus was in the stern, sleeping on a cushion. The disciples woke him and said to him, "Teacher, don't you care if we drown?"

He got up, rebuked the wind and said to the waves, "Quiet! Be still!" The wind died down, and it was completely calm.

He said to his disciples, "Why are you so afraid? Do you still have no faith?" Mark 4: 35-40 (NIV)

Let's give this story some proper perspective. These aren't the days of fiberglass boats with 400 horsepower engines and navigation systems. Most likely, these men are in a boat made of wood and powered by the wind and oars—wind mind you, that is now tossing this boat around like a piece of driftwood floating in the water. Clearly, the body of water they are on is large enough that the storm has placed them in grave danger because it terrified them. It's obvious they weren't able to just row to shore and save the day. And it's doubtful they had life vests.

It's also important to keep in mind that some of these men, before becoming disciples of Jesus, were professional fishermen which means they have significant experience with boats and being on the water. Most likely they've seen plenty of storms during their days on the water, but this one has them convinced they're about to die.

There is great fear.

Emotions are on overload. The scene is no doubt chaotic. Stress and anxiety run high. It's reasonable to assume there's a lot of shouting and screaming about how to maneuver the boat to avoid capsizing. Everyone is hoping someone else knows what to do to save them all before it's too late. It doesn't get much darker when you're on the verge of drowning.

But during all this chaos, Jesus is... sleeping...

While everyone else is desperately trying to save their lives, Jesus is peacefully asleep, unaffected by the storm or the chaos all around him. This is where anger probably enters the story. We can feel it in the words of the disciple who asked, "Don't you care if we drown?"

Like any dramatic, high stakes story, there's a last-minute rescue that saves them all. But it doesn't come from the coast guard that arrives just in time, or a helicopter that plucks them from the boat, or an unexpected island that appears. Rescue occurs in the form of words spoken directly to the storm.

Words.

That's the rescue that comes when you're on a wooden boat,
in the middle of the sea,
in a deadly storm,
with the Son of God on board.

We can all relate to this story because most of us have been in this storm. Darkness came quickly and unexpectedly, like a sudden storm that swept in and brought fear and threat. We know what the disciples felt because we've felt that fear. Maybe you weren't fearful that you would die, but the pain and agony may have felt like death. We understand what it's like to be at the end of our rope—we tried everything to rescue ourselves but the wind kept blowing and the waves kept crashing over our boat. We know that helpless feeling of having no control and being at the mercy of the storm. I suspect, in our own way, we even cried out to God, "Don't you care if I drown? Do you not see the situation I'm in, God? Are you asleep?"

"WAKE UP AND SAVE ME," we cry out in the middle of
the chaos.

In our darkest moments, whether we turn to God immediately or
after we've tried and failed in our own rescue attempt, we turn to God
eventually and plead, beg even, for him to save us from the storm. We
want him to speak into our storm and quiet the wind and calm the
waves. It's late in the movie of our life and we need the last-minute,
heroic rescue—

and we expect,
demand even,
that God deliver.

I think we miss the point of this story. Like the disciples, we're
focused on what we want Jesus to do for us. In our fear, all we can see
is we're out of options and Jesus is our last hope for rescue. After all, if
he can tame the wind and sea, surely, he can fix our marriage, or save
our child from drug addiction, or repair our broken heart, or cure my
cancer.

- But what about the times when God hasn't delivered the
  rescue we desired?
- Did God remain asleep on a cushion in the boat while the
  storm ravaged our lives?
- Did he not care that we drowned?
- Did God choose to not show up to save us?

When he doesn't show up the way we expect or hope, we're often left wondering why. We may even become angry and blame God for failing to rescue us, failing to calm the storm, letting us down. How can a good God save some from their storm while it seems he stays asleep during others' storms? There's one more verse to this story:

> "They were terrified and asked each other, 'Who is this?
> Even the wind and waves obey him.'" —Mark 4:41

We find the gem in this last verse. The disciples' first reaction isn't relief that he saved them. It isn't even gratitude toward their rescuer. The disciples' first response is awe. They've just witnessed the wind and the waves stilled by the mere spoken words from their teacher, rabbi, friend.

> Imagine this scene.
> Jesus awakes,
> speaks to the wrath of nature,
> and nature not only listens
> but obeys his commands.

> Dwell on this for a moment.

Often, I think we're more interested in what we want God to do for us, than what He has already done for us. We focus more on what he can do than who he is. That's why we miss the depth of this story. Our focus is on what he did here—he stopped the storm and saved the day.

But I think the main point of this story
is not what God did here,
but who God proved himself to be.

If even the wind and waves obey his very words,
how much more can we trust him with our lives?

Which means we need to ask ourselves the hard question—am I willing to trust the God who controls the wind and waves with the storms of my life, even if he chooses not to calm my storm?

In the early days following my cancer diagnosis, when fear was raging like a perfect storm, I was like the disciples in the boat, crying out for rescue. My gale force wind and twenty-foot waves were a rare, incurable cancer. My boat was taking on water, and chaos surrounded me. Hope was fading fast. Rescue appeared unlikely. I was calling out to God to wake up. "Don't you see I'm drowning here?" I pleaded.

A Challenge, a Shift, and My Choice

It was during the days after my diagnosis, but before surgery. I felt weak in my faith, ashamed that I couldn't control the fear. I pleaded with God for strength, for the courage to trust him with this storm, yet wondering if he was still asleep.

On a cold winter morning, while driving to work, and listening for something, anything from God that I could attach my trust to, his answer came in the form of a challenge: God was asking me to trust him completely... or walk away from him for good. Sounds harsh, I realize. But I'm confident this was God's response to my cries for him to quiet my storm and calm my fear.

Do you trust me, Bill?

Do you trust me with your cancer?

Do you trust me with the results?

Do you trust me with your life?

My Sunday school answer was clear:

"Of course, I trust you God. You know I trust you. I've been your follower for years."

My Sunday school answers didn't work for me—or for God.

He came at me again.

"No, do you trust me even if I decide not to stop this storm?"

Did you just feel the weight of that question I felt that day?

It was clear. Trusting God fully in this moment meant I would have to trust his plan, even if that meant I would die from this cancer. But this trust would require that I completely accept the results, knowing the God who controls the winds and the waves had a better plan for my life than I did, even if that meant this storm wouldn't be stopped.

Trusting God had just taken on an entirely new meaning.

This was no longer the warm, fuzzy kind of trust learned from stories in vacation Bible school, when Jesus had long, blond hair, blue eyes and wore a white robe with a blue sash. This was a trust that was real and raw and existed at a place within my soul I'd never been.

It was a trust that was terrifying,
yet inexplicably comforting.

Yet it was also a point of no return: God was saying that if I didn't choose to trust him at this level, that I had no place with him any longer.

It's a remarkable thing to tell the God of the universe
it's okay if he ends your life.
Yet, that is exactly what I did.
As if my permission was required,
I granted it.

You see, I knew that just as Jesus stilled the winds and calmed the sea for the disciples, he could do the same for me. But this decision to trust God was more about trusting him for who he is rather than what he can do.

I decided I was more interested in trusting God
because of his power *over* the wind and the sea
than his choice to act *upon* the wind and the sea.

This decision required that I shift my thinking about God and choose to trust him differently than ever before. I had to shift from thinking about what God can do for me and choose to trust what God has already done for me. And it was a choice to trust God for who he is and for no other reason. It was a choice that reshaped my faith.

It always comes down to a choice, doesn't it?

Your storms are every bit as dark as mine—maybe even darker. Yet, while it seems the storms come to tear us down, God can use them to build us up and restore, sometimes reshape, our faith. God is always there, in the boat with us, waiting for us to trust him, asking "Why are you so afraid? Do you still have no faith?" In the end, it's not as important what he does with the wind and the waves as it is that he is there in the boat holding us with a firm grip, even if we think he's asleep.

05

A Better Way of Being Human

Deeper than our instinct to live is our longing to be alive.[1]
—Erwin McManus

A few years have passed since the events I described in the last couple chapters. Time moved on. So did my life. But living through a dark storm leaves its imprint. We're changed. No matter how hard we try, it's almost impossible to return to "normal life," whatever that was. Moving forward feels different, awkward even.

No matter your circumstances the question is the same:

Now what?

The question gives expression to our lament, carries our pain, our grief, and our loss as we wonder what life will look like now. It gives language to our fear of an uncertain and unknown future. It cries out for a light to illuminate our next step because our foothold feels unsteady and our direction unclear.

We survived the storm.

We're still here.

So, now what?

As I explored the answer to this question during my space in between, my soul continued to return to that Isaiah 41:10 verse in the 'Take Courage' cards I carried in my pocket for so long. My mind kept repeating the last line—that last promise; "I'll hold you steady, keep a firm grip on you." I clung to the words "firm grip" with an ever-increasing confidence that I wasn't alone, that I didn't have to discover the answer to the question, 'now what?' by myself.

I began to sense that the question hints at the future. There's something next, something more, and that I have the ability to make choices in how I step in to what's next. God's promised "firm grip" on my life turned 'now what?' into a Divine signpost of sorts that leaned toward hope, suggesting a new path forward. As the promise of "firm grip" began to shape my life more each day, the question, 'now what?' gradually morphed into a new question:

Now, how do I want to live?

That's a big question, isn't it? I thought so too. You can feel the weight of a question like this. It's heavy. It has depth and texture. If you could hold a question like this in your hand, you'd hold it tightly, protect it, keep it safe because it suggests so many possibilities.

It seemed a question this big demanded an equally big answer. After all, this question wasn't asking how I wanted to live regarding my career, or geographic location, or what hobbies I wanted to pursue. It's asking what values I want to inform my life, what gives my life meaning, and how I want to be remembered when I'm gone.

I didn't know where to start. It required time and intention. It would take thought and reflection on how I'd lived to that point, and what I wanted to be different in the future. So, I decided to start with just one day—to choose how I wanted to live for one day. And then I did the same thing the next day. And the day after that, day after day. As I reflected during that season of my life, one theme continued to emerge—two words that shaped my thoughts, choices, who I was becoming, and how I lived those days—firm grip.

God's promise to hold me in his firm grip became a cornerstone on which I created my life. The words 'firm grip' began to shape everything in my life, knowing that if I was held in the firm grip of the One who created me, I can live in confidence.

Firm-grip became the big answer to that big question.
Firm-grip became the new way I wanted to live my life.
And the firm-grip life is what I've lived since.

What is the Firm-Grip Life?

If best-selling author and research professor, Brené Brown, asked me, as she asks guests on her podcast, to describe a snapshot of an ordinary moment in my life that brings joy, my answer would come easily: Being with Jane on a weekend morning, sipping lattes, reading, and talking about anything, or nothing at all. In that ordinary moment, I need nothing else. My world is right. In that moment, I experience a clear sense of confidence, peace, and calm. I don't know why I feel that way, but I know I do.

I suspect you know exactly what I'm saying. You have places, or people, or experiences that put you in that similar vibe where your stars align perfectly, where your confidence is strong and you know only peace. It's something you feel in your soul, a place you wish you could remain forever. It's hard to describe, isn't it?

But you know it's real,
because you've been there.

There are things we know, and then, there are things we *know*. We know that every day our bodies require food, shelter, and sleep. We know that if we step on the gas pedal, the car will move. We know that if we pet a barking dog, it might bite. We know these things because we've experienced them and they're easy to explain. But then there are other things we know, that are difficult to explain—real experiences that seem to escape logic or rational thought.

Yet, we still *know* they are real.

Do you remember when you met your spouse or significant other? You dated for a while, but at some point, the relationship pivoted. You felt things you hadn't felt in other relationships. Then one day, you *knew* this person was the one. If asked, you couldn't explain how you knew this person was the one, all you could say was you *knew*. And you did.

Somehow, you *knew*.

If you're a parent, think back to the first time you held your baby. It was magical. You couldn't believe how much you instantly loved this little life. You'd known love, but not *this* kind of love. This was new. This was a love deeper than any love you imagined possible. This love would do anything to protect this little one. Yet, there's no way you'd be able to explain how this love was different than the love you've previously experienced.

But it was, and you *knew*.

Do you remember when you first discovered a career or passion you loved? You don't really know why you loved it so much or how it was different than other jobs or interests you've pursued, but somehow, your soul was stirred. You felt alive. Something clicked inside you that lit you up. You knew this was your calling, that this was what you were supposed to do with your life. Trying to tell someone why you felt this way would be impossible, wouldn't it?

But you just *knew*.

If we attempted to describe how we *know* these things, it'd be like trying to describe the taste of water, or explain how we can feel music. You might successfully illuminate some of its elements, but the life behind them remains a mystery. But that doesn't matter, or change our reality, does it?

We have an intuitive, deeper way of *knowing*.
Informed by Spirit, *we... just... know*.

The firm-grip life is like that.
Difficult to explain.
But once I chose to live it, I just *knew*.

"Don't panic. I'm with you. There's no need to fear for I'm
your God.

I'll give you strength. I'll help you. I'll hold you steady,

keep a firm grip on you."

Isaiah 41:10 (The Message)

The firm-grip life embraces the Divine command not to panic. It clings to the promise that Spirit is with us. We're not fending for ourselves in our suffering. God is with us. I don't truly understand what that means at a cellular level, but I know it's true. I don't know how. But I *know*.

The firm-grip life believes that God knows our greatest fears and will take them upon himself for our sake. That Divine love, like a parent's love for a child, will do anything too for its beloved. How do I know that? I just *know*.

The firm-grip life trusts that God grants strength when we've lost ours, and help when we're helpless to help ourselves. In unending abundance. Every moment of every day. In every circumstance we face. With every breath we take. I can't prove this. But I *know*.

The firm-grip life believes we have great hope, at all times, and especially in our darkest storms because God is steady and his grip is firm. All the time. No matter what. The firm-grip life declares this to be true. This, I *know*.

The firm-grip life is grounded in faith,

informs our thoughts,

inspires our choices,

and orients our soul toward hope.

Because what we orient ourselves toward, we become.

When we choose to orient our soul to hope instead of despair, we cultivate a mental environment more inclined toward positive thinking and gain the courage to make new choices that create a more positive life and hopeful future.

We begin to *know* the firm-grip life.

During my space in between, I began to live differently, intentionally embracing my deeper *knowing* that I was held in a firm grip of Divine proportion. The passage of five decades of life had already begun a shift in my thinking even before my diagnosis. I had already noticed that acquiring possessions lost its luster, the pursuit of wealth had become meaningless. It was a gradual shift that had been occurring over several years. Then my MTC diagnosis arrived. That changed everything. Not only was my physical health, even my life, in danger, but so was the future I was building for myself and my family. But as I worked through the mind games that cancer played, I gained a much clearer view of my life, in the present and the future.

Shortly after my surgery, I heard a song by a favorite indie band, The Rocketboys, that said, "Time is all we have, and I am just collecting."[2] And that's what I became—a collector. A collector of experiences, memories, and cherished time with family and friends. I became more interested in doing things than buying things— in making memories than making deposits in my bank account. I embraced time with Jane, my sons, and dear friends, sharing life together. I developed a longing to do things I hadn't done and go places I hadn't been. A deepened desire to connect more intimately with my Creator arose. I became clear-focused on living intentionally aware of each day, each hour, each moment even, not letting anything slip past unnoticed and unappreciated.

As the song continued, "We are like ice in water,"[3] here for a moment, then the moment is gone. I decided I wouldn't waste a moment. I chose to breathe in deeply the fullness that life offers, a fullness that I had too often overlooked in pursuit of meaninglessness. I decided to experience each day as something special, knowing it will never come my way again.

I chose to live the firm-grip life.

At the time, I didn't fully understand what that meant. I'm still figuring it out. In the years since, the firm-grip, positive-focused choices have enhanced all aspects of my life, many of which we'll explore in Part II of this book. The firm-grip life shifted my perspectives, refocused my goals, and granted me new confidence, grounded in a deep *knowing* that if I'm held in God's firm grip, then I'll live with a confident, firm grip on all of life.

Before I go further, it's important I make clear that the firm-grip life is not a band-aid for your wounds and certainly not a magic pill that will fix your life or erase your pain, grief, or the bad memories of your dark storm. It's not a belief system or religion that says if we just have enough faith all will be well. The firm-grip life is not a "fake it until you make it" proposition that pretends everything is fine when your world is falling apart. And it's not a pie in the sky ideology that we have the ability to metaphysically change our circumstances if we just think and live with a positive attitude. I have no unrealistic belief that living a firm-grip life will cure my cancer.

Not everything can be fixed.
Pain doesn't always go away.

Grief doesn't have an end date.

Fear always lurks.

Life will always be hard.

The firm-grip life has nothing to do with fixing these things.

The firm-grip life is about embracing a stubborn hope that we can live in the midst of brokenness and pain with an alternative, intentionally selected mindset to thrive again no matter what we've been through. Because when we live full of stubborn hope everything changes. Relationships improve. We love ourselves and others better. We live in greater confidence of who we are and how we can contribute to a better world.

We live with more grace,

more peace

and a grand hope.

We simply become better humans.

Firm-grip living frees us from needing life to be perfect and allows us to live confidently in the life we have. It's about worrying less and trusting more, fearing less, and living with more courage. The firm-grip life is about holding the fragility of our humanness loosely knowing that our Creator holds us firmly.

The firm-grip life is about living in the space in between and choosing to hang on for dear life, rather than let go, confident that God is in your boat even when it seems he's asleep. Like weekend morning lattes with Jane, firm-grip living is a state of confidence, peace, and calm that *knows* when we're losing our grip, God is strengthening his.

The firm grip life is a state of mind, heart, and soul.

An intentional way of living.

A better way of being human.

How do I know that's true?

I've lived it and I *know*.

Your Firm-Grip Life

If you invited me to your home and gave me a tour, I'd get a good feel for your style and design preferences. I'd probably see glimpses of what's important to you, the hobbies you enjoy, and your taste in art. Your home would put off a vibe that hints at what makes you tick, and a bit about how you live. You wouldn't have to tell me those things— your home would do the talking.

If we sat down and you told me about your family, career, education, background, and interests, I'd learn about your life, how you live and what you do. But if you opened your heart and told me about your greatest hopes, your worst fears, your biggest regrets, your wildest ambitions, what gives you joy, what causes you pain, and the deepest longings of your soul, I would see who you are as a human, how your soul is wired, what stirs you, and what kind of energy your life puts into the world. You wouldn't have to tell me those things, I'd just *know*.

Our souls have a way of telling the world who we are.

Just as our homes have an ethos, a feeling of a certain kind of environment, our lives project an ethos, a vibe, a spirit, based on our mindset and attitudes that impact everything we do and every relationship we experience. The firm-grip life is about intentionally choosing a mindset and attitude, the vibe we put out into the world, the ethos that defines our energy—a negative energy or a positive energy.

What vibe does your life put out?
Deep down, you *know.*

The rest of this book is an invitation to choose to live a firm-grip, positive life narrative. If you believe in the God of my faith, the One I write about in the pages of this book, you have the same foundation as mine from which to begin to live your firm-grip life.

Maybe you aren't sure about the God I describe here but have some gut feeling that there is a higher being, something, someone, somewhere that has some bearing on what happens to you and this world. Start there. Launch your firm-grip life from that place of deep *knowing* that exists within you.

You may believe we're in this life alone, on our own to figure it out as we go. That's okay too. You can still choose to shift your thoughts, and make new choices that will point your life to a more hopeful future. Start your firm-grip life from the truth that you can make intentional decisions about your mindset and attitudes toward the life you live. You just might discover along the way that you're not as alone as you thought.

From whatever starting point you step into the firm-grip life, remember it's more about your intentions than your perfections. It's about paying attention to your thoughts and the choices you make throughout your day, with a focus on hope. And it's much more about your direction than a destination.

I didn't choose the firm-grip life because I didn't die.
I chose the firm-grip life because I wanted to fully live.
Read that again— there's a big difference.

Have the dark storms of your life left you stuck, asking yourself "Now what?" over and over? Do the fears of your past keep you from creating a better, more positive and hopeful future? Do you long for more? Does your life always feel like it's one step away from something better? Maybe it's time to move on to the next question:

Now *how* do you want to live?

You have a choice. I urge you to consider choosing to live the firm-grip life. How will you know if you're living it? Oh, you'll know. You'll definitely *know*. But your first step is to act.

06

While There's Still Time

The most difficult thing is the decision to act, the rest is merely tenacity.
—Amelia Earhart

Few of us think about the end of our lives often. Hopefully, that's because we're too busy living to think about dying. But I suspect it may also be in part because we've lulled ourselves with the belief that we have plenty of time left. We're accustomed to the idea that most people get about eighty years on Earth before the last grain of sand drops through the hourglass. If we're lucky, we might even squeeze out another decade. The younger we are, the further away those final years seem. So, we live life convinced there will always be time later for the important stuff. Urgency can wait.

Periodically, we're reminded life doesn't always go as planned. The news tells of tragic accidents, cancer diagnoses, and other unexpected events that end the lives of people far younger than expected. But most of the time, those stories are about someone you don't know, affecting people you've never met. I call it the "Someone Else Syndrome." As long as it's someone else, it really has no meaningful impact on us. So, we scroll to the next story in our news feed, not giving much thought.

People on their deathbed frequently reflect on their life, share stories of the good times, and talk about their regrets. Hospice nurses hear the dying express what they wish they'd done differently while there was still time. The regrets are very similar from person to person.

I wish I would have worked less and spent more time with
my family.
I wish I would have stayed in touch with friends.
I wish I had been happier and enjoyed life more.
I wish I had taken better care of myself.
I wish I had pursued my passions.
I wish I had cared less about what others think.

I'm sure we could make a list now, even with many years of life left (there I go assuming again), of what we'd like to do over, making different choices the next time around. I'll bet if we made that list, it wouldn't include wishes for big houses, fancy cars, or more clothes in the closet. Rather, I suspect our list would reveal a longing for…

more love in our relationships,
more time with family and friends,
less stress and anxiety,
more attention to self-care,
more gratitude,
deeper faith,
a slower pace,
a kinder and generous heart,

more contentment,

more peace,

and more joy.

Add your deepest longings to this list.

I bet they don't have anything to do with the balance in

your bank account.

Besides our ability to make a list, we have something else in common with the dying. We suffer from the same condition that birthed their regrets—failure to act. Like the dying, we've failed to make the choice to act. Stop for a moment and read again the list of the regrets of the dying. Then read again the list of what I suspect we might include now.

See what I mean?

Failure to act by failing to make new choices created these regrets.

While it might be true that many situations improve, it's not because of time, it's because of intention. Intentional action to make new choices can avoid every regret on both lists. When we don't act, we choose to remain in the same place. Unfortunately, the dead ran out of grains of sand. If you're reading this, you still have sand left, at least for now.

The firm-grip life requires us to act.

Momentum

Choices create momentum.
Good choices create positive momentum.
Bad choices create negative momentum.
Momentum grows.

For example, Kyle has a habit of eating lots of fast food and making poor nutrition choices making Kyle overweight. Kyle's weight makes him feel tired and lethargic. By the end of the workday, Kyle is too exhausted to go to the gym or even take a walk around the neighborhood. So, Kyle goes home, throws a pizza in the oven, and spends the evening on the couch watching television.

Kyle looks in the mirror and is disgusted by his reflection. His self-esteem sinks. He convinces himself no one wants to be around someone like him, so he withdraws from friends and family. Kyle isn't happy with his work and longs for something more fulfilling but is convinced he doesn't have much to offer, so he stays in a job he loathes for the paycheck. As time passes, Kyle believes his life really doesn't matter. Kyle is lonely. He doesn't feel well physically or mentally. He feels stuck. Kyle develops a negative focus on life and is miserable. Every day, he is miserable.

Maybe I exaggerated Kyle's life a bit to make my point, but maybe I didn't.

But here's the biggest problem for Kyle, bigger than eating habits or loneliness: Kyle's poor choices have built negative momentum, making it difficult for him to see anything but negative, feel anything but negative, and think anything but negative. As a result, Kyle is living a negative life with a negative attitude and negative outlook on his future. Unless he interrupts this momentum, it will continue to build.

When poor choices create negative momentum, one negative-focused day rolls into the next negative-focused day, week after week, month after month, until the months become years. When the years become a lifetime, people find themselves on their death bed making a list of regrets.

Fortunately, for those of us not yet on our deathbed, we still have time to shift the way we think to interrupt, reverse even, the negative momentum in our lives. Our friend Kyle can choose to continue in his ways of thinking that have led to his negative-focused life, or he can choose to break the pattern and make new choices that can radically alter his life and his future. If Kyle doesn't intentionally choose to shift the way he thinks and take action by making new choices, why would Kyle ever expect tomorrow to look any different from today?

Taking action to live the firm-grip life is a choice.

Firm-Grip Life Markers

It doesn't matter how the dark days and difficult times arrived in your life. Maybe you were the unfortunate recipient of difficult trials through no choice or action of your own. You didn't have any say in the other driver crossing the centerline. No one asked you if the COVID-19 pandemic would turn your world upside down. You couldn't stop time from running out when your loved one died.

Or like Kyle, maybe you made some poor, seemingly insignificant, choices that created problems and struggles that now feel like a weight on your soul, pulling you deeper and deeper into the abyss of negativity.

Either way, you can take action by making new choices now to live the firm-grip life that builds positive momentum and creates a hopeful future.

The reality is that living a positive-focused, firm-grip life is the result of many small daily choices (ones that may even feel insignificant at the time) that build positive momentum. The more positive momentum we build, the easier it becomes to wake each day and choose a positive attitude that creates a better future.

In Part I of this book, we've examined the importance of shifting the way we think about our circumstances and the power we have to choose to respond differently, positively, and with hope based on faith in a God who is always with us, always for us and holds us in his firm grip. As I began to live the firm-grip life, I discovered life markers that help me gauge if I'm making choices that affirm the firm-grip life. Like tumor markers in my blood identify cancer activity, life markers help me see how I'm living, and where I need to shift my thoughts and make new choices to better live the firm-grip life.

In Part II, we'll look at some life markers to see how shifting our thoughts and making new choices in some basic, everyday aspects of life can help us live the firm-grip life. Certainly, I've not identified every life marker that affects everyone. No doubt there are markers in your life that are difficult for you that I won't address here. But I hope learning to think this way will encourage you to make some new choices that point you to the firm-grip life.

A word of caution: You may resonate with much of what we address in the coming pages. You might even identify many new choices you wish to make to improve your life and cultivate new thought patterns that will grow into firm-grip living. But start slow. Choose a couple of areas to change and take confident, committed steps toward those new choices. As you experience success with your new choices, move on to a few more new choices and implement those.

Living the firm-grip life is a marathon, not a sprint. So is making new, positive choices. You can't shift your entire mindset and make all new choices overnight. Besides, the journey you are about to take is far too beautiful to rush. You need to savor every step as you go.

If this sounds like self-help, it is. But this self-help is not void of faith because I believe real faith requires us to take action to create firm-grip lives. Asking God to give us a firm-grip life is the wrong prayer. The right prayer is to ask God to give us the strength, courage, resolve, and determination to take action and make new choices that create a positive-focused, firm-grip life and a hopeful future. Nothing requires more faith in and dependence on the Divine than deciding to shift the way you think and make new choices. But faith without action is like an electrical cord without a power outlet. Both only work when we take action to plug in and tap the power.

Finally, let me say I've not perfected each of these life markers myself. Like you, some of these chapters take on life issues I'm doing well with while others are an ongoing struggle for me. I'll be honest with you along the way and tell you where I struggle most. But hopefully, together we can learn new ways to think that point us to better choices that improve our lives. Since our end goal is to live the firm-grip life with an increased positive focus, each decision we make and each step we take will either help clear the path to our goal or place more obstacles in our way. It's my hope that by the end of this book we have cleared our paths wide open to embrace the firm-grip life.

Could you imagine reaching the end of your life,
sitting down to write your list of regrets
and coming up blank?
It's possible.
But you have to act.

PART II

The Firm-Grip Lifestyle

07

It Is What It Is

_____

Life Marker: Acceptance

Getting over a painful experience is much like crossing monkey bars. You have to let go at some point to move forward.
—C.S. Lewis

On April 15, 2013, Rebekah Gregory stood near the finish line at the Boston Marathon to cheer for a friend in the race. Before any celebration began, a terrorist's bomb exploded sending shrapnel through Rebekah's left leg. She endured dozens of surgeries and suffered horrific pain and deep emotional wounds. Nineteen months later, the doctors amputated her leg. It'll take the rest of her life to work through the emotional damage. But Rebekah was determined to rebuild her life. After learning to walk with a prosthetic leg, even run again, Rebekah returned to the Boston Marathon, where she ran part of the course.

Nick Vujicic was born in 1982 with tetra-amelia syndrome, a rare disorder characterized by the absence of all limbs. Bullied as a child, he attempted suicide at age ten. At age seventeen, after reading about another disabled man who refused to allow his limitations to dictate his life, Nick chose to abandon self-pity and took control of his life. Freed from years of negative thought patterns, Nick's life truly began. He graduated from college with degrees in accounting and finance. Since then, Nick launched a non-profit organization, started a company called Attitude is Altitude, starred in a film, and authored the book, *"Life Without Limits: Inspiration for a Ridiculously Good Life."*

At age thirteen, Bethany Hamilton was a promising young surfer living in Hawaii, a professional surfing career her destiny. But on October 31, 2003, a fourteen-foot tiger shark attacked Bethany, severing her left arm at the shoulder. Only thirty days after the attack, she got back on a surfboard. Teaching herself to surf with one arm, Bethany won a national championship in 2005 and began competing on the professional circuit in 2007. In 2004 she won an ESPY Award for Best Comeback Athlete. Her story became the subject of a documentary film in 2007 and a big-screen movie in 2011 called, *"Soul Surfer."*

My friend Dave was twenty years old when he was thrown from his motorcycle while crossing railroad tracks. He landed on his head, causing a T5-T7 compression fracture resulting in permanent paralysis from his sternum down. In college at the time of his accident, Dave finished school, earning his bachelor's degree. Despite confinement to a wheelchair, Dave moved forward.

He started a business called The Wheel Chair Shop that provides paralyzed clients the opportunity to re-engage life. Besides offering various wheelchairs and medical devices, Dave's business modifies homes, automobiles, and RVs to allow his clients to live with mobility, even affording paraplegics the opportunity to drive vehicles, opening doors of access to life.

Dave joined the Chicago Cubs-sponsored wheelchair softball team and traveled nationally, playing first base and earning all-tournament honors twice during the National Wheelchair Association Tournament. Dave's held national rankings as high as first in doubles and second in singles in the United States Tennis Association's Wheelchair Class A Division. Oh, and in his spare time, Dave has fully restored seven muscle cars.

We all love real-life stories like these. We're intrigued by the struggle and captivated by the ability to overcome. These stories offer hope to people dealing with their own darkness and motivation and courage to find a path through the dark and back to something that resembles a normal life. When we read these stories it's easy to imagine ourselves in their place and wonder, "Would I have the courage to overcome that kind of darkness?" We tell ourselves, "If that person can handle that, then I can handle this, right? After all, my dark isn't nearly as challenging."

Yet despite our desire to move on with our lives, to rise above our pain, to reclaim our lives again, far too often we find ourselves unable to overcome our darkness. As a result, our pain continues, fear remains, and life stands still. Unable to move forward, we're stuck in the dark. And what's worst is the feeling it will never change, that the dark is our final destiny.

I'm confident Rebekah, Nick, Bethany, and Dave each had many factors that helped them overcome the darkest days of their lives, but they all had at least one thing in common that allowed them to not only move forward but propelled them to create vibrant, hopeful lives.

At some point in their darkest days, there was a moment, a specific time that each of them chose to take their first step to accept their circumstance.

It may have been through tears, an angry outburst, or even during the depths of self-pity and despair, but they each reached the place where they told themselves: *it is what it is, but it will not define me.*

The ability to overcome our darkest days and most difficult struggles must begin with accepting our situation for what it is. If we never allow ourselves to accept it for what it is, the journey to overcome can never begin. We will remain stuck with our pain, fear, despair, grief, anger, brokenness, and hopelessness day after day.

It's difficult to wake each day and choose to live the firm-grip life with yesterday's struggles and problems perched on our bedpost waiting to greet us each morning: "Hey you. I'm still here and you have to deal with me again today."

Yet that's how we live far too often and for far too long. Life throws us that two-strike curveball—the death of a loved one, a miscarriage, or a worldwide pandemic. Or maybe we swung at some bad pitches on our own when we mismanaged our finances and put the family in crisis or were unfaithful to our spouse and lost our family. Whatever the circumstance and no matter the means of its arrival in our life, until we take the step toward accepting it for what it is, we can never overcome it and move forward with life. We will be a prisoner of our own minds, refusing to accept reality as it is.

Our misconception of our reality is one reason we get stuck and struggle to accept our darkness for what it is. We have this idea of how things are supposed to be. Then life happens, darkness shows up, and completely ruins our plans.

- Where did we get the idea of how life is supposed to be?
- Why do we presume life will happen according to our plans?
- And why are we always shocked when life goes wrong?

Here's the reality:
There is no such thing as the way things should be.
There is only the way things are.

Groundhog Day

When you refuse to accept the reality of your circumstances, you spend an excessive amount of time and energy trying to undo something you can't undo. Whatever it is, it happened. You can't change that it happened. No amount of energy you invest in fear, worry, pain, anger, or regret will ever change that it happened. Yet, when you refuse to accept it for what it is, you get stuck living it day after day after day. Throughout the day you think about it, dwell on it, fret over it, wish it hadn't happened, wonder "why me?" and tell yourself how unfair it is. Despite all the energy burned thinking about it, nothing changes.

If you allow it, this pattern will continue until your days turn into years, years wasted on wishing you could undo the past.

I'm reminded of the movie Groundhog Day in which Bill Murray's character relived the same day over and over for eight years, trying to get it right. Have you wasted years of your life wishing to go back to get it right? Have you lost time refusing to accept something that happened in your life? Are you waking day after day, clinging to what happened, refusing to let go, stuck in your Groundhog Day?

It's time to accept that it is what it is
and free yourself to live again, to thrive.

A Hopeful Collision

Let's be clear—accepting the reality of your dark circumstance won't happen immediately. It'll take time. You'll suffer first. When darkness arrives, it always hurts. Our emotions and feelings are part of what it means to live the experience of being human. You'll have a buffet of emotions to choose from that will cause all sorts of pain and angst and turmoil… for a while. Lament always precedes acceptance. Without lament, there can be no true acceptance. But acceptance is ultimately found at the intersection where lament and hope collide. No matter how dark it is, it's in this intersection where you will have to choose to turn toward acceptance of your reality and move forward or dwell on how life was supposed to be and linger in despair.

The firm-grip life is always about choices.
Acceptance is a choice.

After my cancer diagnosis, Jane asked the doctor how worried we should be. He said, "medium worried," with a more than "medium worried" expression on his face. I'm not exactly sure what medium worried looks or feels like. I assure you that when you're told your type of cancer is incurable, medium worried isn't on the list of options. There is only "no worry" or "max worry." I went with max worry while my emotions went on overdrive. They were very real, very raw, and relentless. For days I could not escape my emotions. They were there waiting for me first thing every morning, my constant companion.

I was filled with anxious, emotion-driven questions: Do I need to make a bucket list? Will I be sick and bedridden? Will I be able to keep working? And the big one—how long do I have?

I'm not ashamed or embarrassed that I experienced those emotions. I had to go through them. They were simply part of my humanness, my lament, my process of dealing with something very dark, frightening, and uncertain. But I also knew I couldn't live in those emotions forever—that's not a sustainable way of life. After being reminded that the God who controlled the wind and the waves with his words had me in his firm grip, I knew it was time to shift my thinking about my cancer and choose to accept its reality no matter how dark it was.

It is what it is.

Accepting life as it is, even the darkness, isn't about denying your feelings and emotions. It's quite the opposite. Acceptance is about transcending and including your emotions. It's about embracing those emotions of fear, anger, pain, sorrow, hurt, and anything else you feel. It's about opening space to acknowledge those emotions, sitting with them, and being honest about your pain. And then allowing that process to slowly change you, shape you, teach you, move you toward the intersection of lament and hope.

Acceptance is about opening yourself
to the suffering
to create the path to move forward.
There is no going back from suffering—
there is only going through.

No White Flags

I don't like my cancer. I didn't like the diagnosis when it came and I don't enjoy living with the uncertainty of it now. There's nothing about it I like. Cancer is an evil disease. And I assure you I will do everything possible to keep it from killing me. Accepting the reality of our dark circumstances doesn't mean that we like the situation nor does it mean we can't continue to work to improve or change the circumstance if possible.

Acceptance isn't about rolling over in surrender. It's about rising in courage, strength, and determination to live again, believing our best is yet to come. Acceptance is choosing hopefulness—instead of hopelessness—in a newfound freedom to live again. Accepting our reality is simply choosing to be okay with it, accepting the truth of our life, and freeing ourselves to lean forward into a better future that isn't haunted by the past.

Accepting our reality is loving ourselves
enough to say it is what it is,
while refusing to let it define us.

I am not that cancer.
I am not that divorce.

I am not that mistake.
I am not that failure.
I am not that loss.
And I refuse to carry the burden of that identity for one
more day.

Make no mistake—even after acceptance comes the battle to remain in acceptance. But accepting your darkness for what it is today, gives you the courage to accept it tomorrow and the day after that… and the day after that… and the day after that… each new day a renewed choice to live forward into acceptance.

The firm-grip life gives us the strength and courage to choose acceptance.

Unexpected Gifts

Although I muttered to myself, "I have cancer," when the doctor's office called to accelerate my appointment, deep down, it wasn't real to me. Even after being told of my diagnosis, it didn't sink in. I lived in denial of this new reality for a long time, somehow thinking a new day might bring a miracle and the cancer had magically disappeared. It was a couple of months before I could begin the journey to acceptance. My first step is recorded in a journal entry that reads as follows:

"I have cancer. There. I wrote it. It has taken me sixty-eight days to write it.

I've said the words several times. But those words vanished into the air, gone like vapor.

I've written those words in some texts and emails, but those were easily deleted and no longer stared back at me on the screen. But to write those words in a journal like this seems so permanent and final. But I need to tell this story even if no one ever reads it.

Telling this story here is therapeutic for me and if nothing else will document the grace and mercy God has shown me during these hard days."

Lament and hope collided.
That was my first step toward acceptance.
That was the first time I acknowledged it is what it is.

When I chose to accept my cancer for what it was, something beautiful and unexpected happened. I created space to discover the gifts God was bringing into my life.

Yes, I said gifts.
Choosing to accept my cancer brought gifts into my life.
It's through our darkest times that God does his greatest work in us.

It's through our trials we come to the place he wanted us all along—trusting and depending on his firm grip.

Unexpectedly, I began to see good things that came with my cancer. The way I related to my Creator changed. My relationship with God became simple, yet very clear. All my prior understandings of the Divine, all my previous beliefs made sense and seemed simple.

It all became clear in an image I saw in my mind in the earliest days after my diagnosis when I envisioned Christ next to me, one hand firmly gripping my arm, his other wrapped tightly, yet gently around my other shoulder. I had that image in my mind's eye every day, during every hospital visit, doctor appointment, every test and procedure, and each step I took through this cancer journey. It was God's way of telling me, "I'm here. I've got my firm grip on you and I'm never letting go. You are not alone. I will be here every step. And when you've no strength left; I'll hold you up."

The treasure was in understanding that God's love for me was more important than the results or outcome, even if that meant the end of my physical life. I have no words to describe the peace that came with this deepened connection to the Divine. That peace helped me accept my circumstances and shift my perspectives.

I no longer sweat the small annoyances of life that previously aggravated me (or at least I'm trying—ask Jane). I now appreciate small but beautiful parts of life I previously overlooked—

The perfect line in a song,
the lingering pleasure from a well-crafted wine,
the sounds of life in a coffee shop,
the embrace of a friend,
an inspiring book,
the piece of art that catches the light just so,
the beauty of the forest out my window,
preparing a meal with my wife.

I now observe all these experiences with a deepened appreciation.

I've often thought how I'd prefer to send the cancer and its uncertainty back to where it came from. But I would never release the gifts that came with my diagnosis. And I'm aware I'd have missed these gifts had I chosen to remain in my darkness, refusing to accept this cancer for what it is.

It is what it is.

When I allowed fear and worry to control, when stress and anxiety drove my emotions, when I could see nothing but despair and self-pity and when chaos occupied my headspace, I had no ability to see what God was doing in my life, how he planned to bless me in ways unimaginable through the trials of my dark days.

- Who knew that an incurable cancer diagnosis could create so much beauty in my life!?
- Who knew that my darkest days would lead me to the firm-grip life?
- But that's what a God who controls the wind and the waves with his words can do!

What are the gifts waiting for you? Maybe you've never considered the possibility that God could create anything good out of your darkness. Or maybe, your head is still so full of chaos that you can't yet see beyond your pain and fear. You don't have to keep living that way. There is freedom from the prison of your own mind. But you have to act. I urge you to shift the way you think and choose to take your first step toward accepting your darkness for what it is.

I don't know what God has waiting for you on the other side of acceptance, but I assure you it is very good. There are gifts waiting for you in the firm-grip lifestyle.

08

It's All a Gift

Life Marker: Gratitude

*No one is as capable of gratitude as one who has emerged
from the kingdom of night.*
—Elie Wiesel

Although the 1970s and 80s produced some of the best music of all time, I don't recall the same success achieved during those decades in the field of cancer treatment and survival. I remember hearing far too many conversations between my parents about their friends who had fallen prey to a cancer diagnosis. I heard talk of surgeries, radiation, chemotherapy, scans, and medical tests. Sometimes, these cancer warriors were the parent of a friend of mine, so I had skin in the game—and a scared friend.

Often, the early treatments produced great results and generated hope for survival, maybe even a cure. I remember seeing them looking well and seemingly back to normal lives after treatment. But I also recall that most of the time, after a couple of years of apparent good health, the phone rang, and I heard my mom's words, and saw the look on her face, and knew the cancer was back. Thinking about those days now, I suspect the evil was probably never fully evicted, but laid dormant, waiting to claim its victim's life later, almost as a cruel joke to have offered false hope. Sadly, most of these folks died after the cancer spread to vital organs.

Modern medical advances altered this scenario; people now live longer with cancer than ever before. But it's hard to check our experiences at the door. So, I brought a mental framework to my fight with the disease, creating a negative platform to launch my battle. With my cancer head-game starting in the hole, I needed to find support and connection to others who knew what the MTC journey entailed. I needed to find a way to create a new mental framework.

More than anything,
I needed to find someone to tell me
I wasn't going to die—
at least not now.

Since MTC is so rare, I knew I wouldn't find an MTC support group at the local American Cancer Society or library, so I turned to the internet. There I discovered the Thyroid Cancer Survivors Association where I also found the MTC medical guidelines, the Bible for treating MTC; but, with the mindset I had, those guidelines only seemed to point to an imminent death. I needed a different kind of support, something more promising. So, I turned to social media where I found a group of people from all around the world who have MTC.

It's a small group considering the rarity of the disease. But there I connected, asked questions, read stories, and heard from others with MTC, already further down the cancer road. I learned that most MTC warriors aren't diagnosed until stage IV since the cancer has very few symptoms, preventing early detection. I didn't know my stage yet.

But my prospects didn't look good.
Negative thoughts raged.

A few weeks later, I awoke early one morning to a cloud of uncertainty and negative thoughts. I grabbed my iPad and turned to my support group, only to find the group mired in sadness. I read that Rebecca, a single mom of a college-aged daughter, had died after a three-year fight with MTC. I didn't know Rebecca. Since I'd been a member of the group for such a short time, we'd not interacted. But in that moment, that didn't matter. I'd just lost a sister. My heart broke for her shortened life and for her daughter.

I couldn't help but wonder if this was the path of all MTC warriors—a mighty battle for a few years, but the same result I witnessed as a child with my parents' friends.

Everywhere I looked, negative thoughts beckoned.
But life's like that, isn't it?
There's always an open seat on the negativity train.

A New Framework

On a particularly difficult day early in my journey, I did something that changed everything. I grabbed a pad of paper and a pen and wrote a list of everyone and everything I was grateful for. I listed family and friends, my faith, and God's grace and mercy. I included my legal career that permitted me to support my family, the opportunity to live in a free country, and all the other blessings in my life I could think of. You know; the important stuff that comes to mind during the rare times we pause long enough to consider what we're grateful for.

I even included my health on the list, maybe as some act of rebellion since I still couldn't believe I had cancer.

Then I went a step further.

I added each person I believed God used in a positive way in this new journey with cancer. I included the names of the medical professionals who had a role in my diagnosis and treatment. The list was long. As I wrote each name and thought of their role in my cancer journey, it became clear that God's hand was in this process from the beginning.

Each person was placed in my life with Divine intentionality.

When I finished, I looked at the list, read through it a few times, and realized something remarkable—my negative thoughts were gone, replaced by thoughts of gratitude. In that moment, despite my uncertain future and so many unanswered questions, I learned one of life's greatest truths—

It's impossible to be negative when my heart is full of gratitude.

I folded that list and carried it in my pocket. Each time negative thoughts called my name, I pulled it out and read it again, opening the door to positive thinking and hope. I continued to add to the list and gratitude became my focus. Gratitude became my new, everyday companion, a gentle reminder that despite the darkness *in* my life, that darkness was *not* my life. Gratitude became my teacher, urging me to shift my gaze beyond my circumstances. Through this learning process, I discovered there are two types of gratitude, each important, but one of them so profound, it can change how we live.

Responsive Gratitude

We've all experienced responsive gratitude—the simple emotion of feeling thankful in response to a positive circumstance. Responsive gratitude flows easily when something good occurs. Landing a new job, receiving a gift, or a visit from a friend will all evoke feelings of thankfulness. Even simple things like someone holding a door for us, buying us a cup of coffee, or bagging our groceries can make us feel thankful—for a moment. Then the moment is gone and so is the feeling. Responsive gratitude is a basic human response (or should be) that is automatic, a feel-good emotion that momentarily lifts our spirit. We don't have to think about responsive gratitude—it just arises but is always based on an external event. Responsive gratitude is a great part of daily life, but rarely will responsive gratitude change our lives.

Intentional Gratitude

Unlike responsive gratitude that arises in response to a pleasant event, we can create gratitude on purpose—with purpose—no matter the circumstances. Intentional gratitude can not only exist in the absence of a positive event but amid negative ones. Intentional gratitude transcends both our feelings and circumstances, often thriving in our worst situations. We can choose gratitude as an intentional mindset in all circumstances.

> We don't have to wait for gratitude to arrive—
> we can pursue it.

Can you imagine experiencing deep gratitude in the midst of your darkest days?

When I created my list of all the people and things I was grateful for, including those who were part of my darkest circumstance, I accidentally stumbled into the territory of intentional gratitude. Understand, this was not a brave and courageous act of intestinal fortitude where I dug deep into my inner strength and fought my way to more positive thoughts. Creating my list, in blunt honesty, was an act of desperation to find some path forward to something more positive than the negativity train I was riding. But what I discovered was that I unintentionally *created* gratitude amid despair. It was impossible to read my list and remain in negative thinking. And I learned that the more I read my list, the greater the intensity of my gratitude grew.

I actually started to get good at gratitude.

Like an athlete trains to improve skills for better performance, we can train ourselves to improve our practice of intentional gratitude. Gratitude, when practiced intentionally, grows in momentum and leads to more gratitude. So, when we intentionally practice gratitude, we improve our skills and become more grateful people. The more gratefully we live, the more positive our thoughts. The more positive our thoughts, the more positive-focused our lives become. It's simply a choice in how we want to live.

So how can we cultivate the discipline of gratitude?

There are as many ways as your imagination will take you, but here's just a few:

1. Create your gratitude list. Write a list of everyone and everything you're grateful for. Carry the list with you. Anytime you sense a negative attitude rising, pull out that list and read it. Return your focus to the good in your life. Add to the list as new people and new experiences offer new opportunities to express gratitude. And don't forget to include the small stuff. Sometimes it's the small stuff that matters most.

2. Start each day with gratitude. First thing each morning, identify one person or thing you'll intentionally focus your gratitude toward that day. Doing so sets the tone for gratitude to flourish throughout the day. You might choose your spouse or significant other, your job, a friend, your kid's teacher, your home, your health, having access to clean water, or medical care. The list is endless. But choose one, and focus on it throughout your day, returning your thoughts as often as possible, reminding yourself amidst the busyness of your day that there is a bigger picture of life than the stress of the moment in front of you.

3. Keep a gratitude journal. If you enjoy writing, keep a journal where you express your gratitude in more detail. Let your imagination explore your thoughts and feelings of gratitude a few days a week. You

can periodically read back through your entries during particularly difficult times for a reminder of your blessings. And imagine the legacy of gratitude you'll pass on one day to your loved ones who read of how you lived with a grateful heart.

4. Take a gratitude walk. Author, speaker, and 'Positivity Hall of Famer,' Jon Gordon encourages thirty-minute gratitude walks when you focus your thoughts on all you're thankful for. As he says, what a great time to get some exercise and express gratitude to the Divine.

5. Just say thank you. As simple as it sounds, saying "thank you" to more people each day will reorient your focus to gratitude. To your boss, the waitress at the diner, the clerk at the store, your spouse, the barista, anyone who does something for you—express your appreciation. Even if they are just doing their job, they've still done something for you. Say thank you and watch your attitude of gratitude increase.

6. Carry an object that reminds you to shift your focus to gratitude. It may be the list you write or some other object that has meaning for you. Put it in your pocket or somewhere you'll come into frequent contact with it. I now carry a small stone in my pocket with the word "Gratitude" etched into it. Whenever I put my hand in my pocket, I feel the stone and I'm reminded to shift my focus back to gratitude, even if only for a moment. I'll think of something or someone from a recent encounter, or I'll recall my cancer journey and focus my gratitude on my current health and stability. Sometimes we just need a reminder to pause and be grateful.

7. Be mindful of the language you use with others and yourself. Are you using positive, encouraging language with others? What words do you speak to yourself? It's difficult to live gratefully when our words are negative.

8. End each day with gratitude. Identify one thing from your day that you're grateful for. It may be something unexpected that occurred during the day, like running into an old friend at the coffee shop. Or maybe it's something bigger, like when I found out my cancer was stage III, not IV. Whatever you identify, whether it's a life-changer or seemingly insignificant, name it and express gratitude for it.

Intentional gratitude is a daily lifestyle practice in the firm-grip life and becomes a core value of how you live. Practicing gratitude restores the soul and the heart into something good and beautiful and right. But it requires daily, active participation. Gratitude, as a discipline, doesn't occur spontaneously. Living in daily gratitude requires an intentional shift in thinking from what is wrong in our lives to all that is right. This practice demands we shift our focus from what we don't have to the abundance that we do have. Practicing gratitude is a shift from the narrow focus of our current darkness to the broader focus on the blessings in our life. These new perspectives help form a new gratitude-based default response to how we see the world, and how we see our lives, even the messy, chaotic, painful, and tragic parts. When we create an active, daily practice of intentional gratitude, living from a place of gratitude becomes our way of life, and we come to realize that...

Gratitude is the bass note of the firm-grip life.

Like the bass drumbeat sets the rhythmic foundation to your favorite songs, gratitude serves as the bedrock found in all the other firm-grip life markers we'll explore in the rest of Part II of this book, because gratitude is where the firm-grip always life starts.

Gratitude is a Choice

It's an inexplicably peaceful feeling to live out an expression of gratitude, even when your world is full of chaos, struggle, and darkness. But it's possible because gratitude is a choice. Gratitude is always a choice. I won't tell you it's always an easy choice when you feel like your world is crashing around you, when you want to shake your fist at the Heavens, and when you feel alone and lost, but I will promise you that choosing to live in an expression of intentional gratitude amidst your darkness will help you shift your perspectives to reframe the way you view your struggles. This is what the firm-grip life is about—finding joy, peace, and hope even in places that previously seemed void of anything good.

I remember a day early in my cancer journey while I was reading my gratitude list when I had these simple, yet paradoxically, monumental thoughts:

It's all a gift.
Nothing is promised.
I get to live this life.

When we recognize all of life as a gift, we can learn to be grateful *in* our suffering, even though we may not be grateful *for* our suffering. But later, when we gain the advantage of intention and the distance of time, we may find that with new eyes and new perspectives, we can actually be grateful *for* our suffering because it led us to changes that helped us create a more positive, hopeful, firm-grip life.

There's a sign in a courtroom I'm in often that reads, "There is always, always, always something to be grateful for." It's a simple truth. So simple that we overlook it every day if we don't choose otherwise. Living gratefully is a choice. The choice is here, now, just waiting for you. Yesterday is in the rearview mirror. Tomorrow is only hoped for. But you have this moment, right now. How will you choose to live it? If you want to create a positive life narrative, you must shift the way you think and make new choices that lead you to a new path, a new way of being in the world, a new path that leads to peace and hope.

Choose gratitude as the bass note of your firm-grip life.

09

Asking the Wrong Questions

Life Marker: Fear

Fear only has as much power as we give it;
hope works the same way.
—Bob Goff

Ask any cancer patient and they'll tell you there are many layers of evil to cancer. The disease itself is an insidious, out-of-control mutation of cells that secretly activates in the body, finds a place to build a home, and begins its sinister voyage of destruction. We only learn this first layer exits when another human in a white coat informs us of the intruder's presence in our body. Those words, "It's cancer," are the second, gut-punching, breath-stealing layer of evil. From there, layer after layer unfolds in the form of never-ending medical tests, surgeries, treatments (which for some can be worse than the cancer itself), feeling sick, missing work, financial stress, loneliness, and more head games than I can list.

Each of these layers presents new opportunities to create fear.

There's another layer of MTC I learned about shortly after my meeting with the guy in the white coat. MTC has a potential genetic component. That means MTC is sporadic (it just happens and you're the only one) or familial (it's hereditary and can be passed through your bloodline).

At the time of my diagnosis, my sons were ages nineteen and twenty-one. The science of MTC says if I had the familial variety of the disease, my sons had a 50% chance of having the genetic mutation for MTC. If that was the case, at their ages, the science also said MTC was likely already growing in the bodies. I've already made clear my fear after my diagnosis, but I held back until now on sharing my deepest fear, the most haunting fear:

I may have passed this cancer to my sons.

They drew a small vial of blood from a vein that had been jabbed with more needles in the past few weeks than the rest of my life combined. I remember staring at it as the technician went about her normal routine of applying a label to the vial. To her it was just another tube of blood evidencing a part of her day's work. To my family, the contents of that glass tube would determine the extent to which my son's lives may forever change.

They sent the blood sample to one of the few labs in the country that performs this unique test. So, we waited... and waited... and waited more. This time of waiting was like sitting in a basement during a tornado, the entire house shaking, not knowing what will happen, but praying the tornado passes. We had no choice but to wait and ride out the storm. Another liminal space of the in between. One thought dominated my mind during those weeks of waiting:

I'd rather lose my life to sporadic MTC
than survive and pass this disease to my sons.

But I didn't get a vote in the outcome.
Fear raged like a hundred-year storm.

Do you ever feel like that? Like your life is a constant battle against fear that you just can't seem to win? Everyone reading this book has experienced fear. But I'll admit I've never experienced fear like I did while I waited to learn if my cancer might have passed to my sons. Having allowed myself to live in the dark valley of fear far too long, I learned something during those days that shifted the way I think and will forever change the way I now choose to live:

It's impossible to create a positive life narrative
when we choose to be consumed by fear.

What If's, Tightropes, and Car Rides

Before we go further, we must understand this—fear isn't always a bad thing. Healthy fear is a normal, human, intuitive response that arises in response to an event or circumstance that puts us in imminent danger. Fear is why we don't walk into a street without looking both ways. Fear keeps us from touching a hot stovetop. Fear prevents us from jumping the fence and petting the lions at the zoo. These rational, beneficial fears require little thought or action; they're an innate, survival response born deep into the human psyche.

But that's not the fear I'm talking about here. You already know the fear I'm referring to in these pages because you've likely lived in its crippling, paralyzing aftermath, the effects of fear that is all-consuming and takes control of your life. Nothing good comes from this kind of fear. When unhealthy fear controls us, it leads to an equally dark place—worry. Worry is the evil twin of fear. When fear and worry tag-team our life, we lose hope. When we lose hope, our thoughts turn dark and our lives become negative.

If we break down fear and worry, we find that the fuel that keeps them in control of our lives is the "what if" questions. During the weeks I awaited the results of my genetic testing, all of my fears and worries came from "what if" questions.

What if I passed a deadly cancer to my sons?
What if it's already started growing?
What if it's already spread to their vital organs?
What if MTC prevents them from graduating from college?
What if they get sick and can't pursue their dreams?
What if it gets aggressive?
What if they die?
What if…. what if…. what if???

You've probably been there, haven't you?

What if my marriage ends?
What if my loved one dies?
What if I lose my job?
What if my kids make bad choices?
What if I fail?
What if no one accepts me?
What if I'm not enough?

These "what if" questions are created by our thoughts—thoughts that are dark, negative and hopeless. But fear and worry are always a product of our thoughts, thoughts that generate a fearful, worrisome response. Here's what I mean.

Cancer itself isn't fear. Cancer is a biological train wreck of cells gone wild that manifests in growth of an undesired tissue in the body. It was my response to cancer that created fear and worry in my life. It was my response to the possibility that I might have passed cancer to my sons that created my worst days controlled by fear and worry.

I created the fear.
I created the worry.

Have you ever considered how often you worry about things that never end up happening? Mark Twain said, "I've lived through some terrible things in my life, some of which actually happened." That's the result when we fill our mind with "what if" questions grounded in fear and worry—we waste energy living negative-focused, worrying about things that will probably never occur.

I spent a couple of months allowing fear-driven "what if" questions to roll around in my head, stealing my hope, robbing my joy, only to learn my blood test revealed my cancer was sporadic and my sons were not in danger. Yet, no amount of fear I created had any impact on that result.

Fear only exists when we breathe life into it
with the thoughts we create.
And guess what?
The thoughts we create
are a choice.

So, if fear is a response we create from thoughts we choose, then we have more control over fear and worry than we realize. Firm-grip living is about embracing that control and claiming the power of our choice over fear.

Nik Wallenda is a member of a multigenerational family of daredevils that has risked his life for decades performing high wire acts. You've probably seen him on TV performing daring stunts. A few years ago, Nik walked a tightrope across the Grand Canyon with no safety harness to prevent a fall to certain death on the canyon floor below. After his courageous canyon walk, Nik was asked how he deals with fear in a profession that risks his life every time he goes to work. "I say it all the time. Fear is a choice, said Nik. You can decide whether you want to be scared or not."[1]

Regardless of what is causing our fear, Nik said we all choose whether we will "allow it (fear) to take root." He said, "As soon as I experience any thought of fear, I kick it out immediately. I always counter negative with positive in every aspect of my life. I truly have no question in my mind that fear is a choice."[2]

Notice that Nik didn't deny the existence of fear. He recognized its presence. He acknowledged it as a choice and admitted fearful thoughts enter his mind. But he doesn't allow those thoughts to stay and occupy his headspace.

He chooses hope over fear, positive over negative.

Even those who appear to have superhero-like courage experience fear. Life is scary no doubt. Fear will always lurk around our lives no matter how brave we think we are. But like everything we're exploring in this book, we have a choice in how we respond. Recognizing the danger of unchecked fear, in her book *Big Magic*, Elizabeth Gilbert speaks directly to fear, warning it, "You're allowed to have a seat, and you're allowed to have a voice, but you are not allowed to have a vote. You're not allowed to touch the road maps; you're not allowed to suggest detours; you're not allowed to fiddle with the temperature. Dude, you're not even allowed to touch the radio. But above all else, my dear old familiar friend, you're absolutely forbidden to drive."[3]

So, for those of us who don't walk tightropes across the Grand Canyon or wear superhero capes, how do we strengthen our resolve to resist fear and worry? How do we shift the way we think about fear, to choose courage over fear? And if courage is nowhere to be found, how can we at least discover a realistic path to hope and peace despite dark circumstances in our lives?

With-ness

So much changed after my cancer diagnosis. One of those changes was how I connected with Jane. At diagnosis, we'd been married twenty-six years. We spent a lot of time together and our marriage was wonderful, but after my diagnosis, I wanted to be with her constantly. I had a fresh perspective on how much I treasured her, but I also had thoughts about how much longer we'd be together. It was hard to leave for work in the morning and I wanted to get home quickly at each day's end to be with her. We laugh now about how each night as we got into bed, I needed to have contact. We have a king-sized bed for a reason—we like our personal space. But during these days, space was the last thing I wanted. She obliged and allowed me to sleep close and with constant contact. There was a peace, a security, a feeling that things would be okay as long as I was close and connected with Jane.

As much as closeness to Jane provided peace in the battle against fear, there was another source—the Source—to which I turned and found my greatest strength. The God of scriptures, the One who created me, the Son who experienced fear in the garden the night before his death on the cross and understands—to that God I turned. Like the fresh perspective with which I connected to Jane, the way I connected to the Divine also transformed. I wanted to be closer. I craved a deeper connection. Although I knew fear was a choice, I also knew that I did not have the strength on my own to choose against it.

Because the real question when we are fearful is...

"God, where are you in this darkness?"

So, I sought my Creator and that answer in the words of scripture. The struggle with fear dates back to the origins of man. The Divine knew the weakness of humans to handle fear. Maybe that's why the Bible has over 300 references to fear with instruction to fear not. But as I read those verses, I noticed something else; I noticed that often, God gave us the reason to not fear—that God was *with* us. Here are just a few of those verses:

> "Be strong. Take courage. Don't be intimidated. Don't give
> them a second thought because God, your God is striding
> ahead of you. He's right there with you. He won't let you
> down; he won't leave you."
> Deuteronomy 31:6 (The Message)

"The Lord is with me; I will not be afraid. What can mere
mortals do to me? The Lord is with me; he is my helper. I
look in triumph on my enemies."
Psalm 118:6-7 (NIV)

"Have I not commanded you? Be strong and courageous.
Do not be afraid; do not be discouraged, for the Lord your
God will be with you wherever you go."
Joshua 1:9 (NIV)

"When you pass through the waters, I will be with you;
And through the rivers, they will not overwhelm you.
When you walk through the fire, you will not be scorched,
nor will the flame burn you."
Isaiah 43:2 (AMP)

"And behold, I am with you always, to the end of the age."
Matthew 28:20 (ESV)

I wanted to be with the Divine but these verses reminded me
that the Divine wanted to be *with* me and was already *with* me. The
strength to choose hope and peace over fear and worry was not to be
found in myself but in the truth that the Creator of all things was *with*
me. I call this the *with-ness* of the Divine. This kind of *with-ness* is not
a warm fuzzy that makes us feel good like a fire on a cold night, but
a *with-ness* that says no matter what you go through, no matter how
terrifying it is, no matter how alone you feel, no matter how hopeless
your life seems, I am *with* you—I am here—I will never leave and you
will never be alone.

As I embraced the *with-ness* of the Divine in my clash with cancer, I came to realize God wasn't telling me to pretend my fear wasn't real, but to trust him despite it. I can acknowledge the presence of fear sitting in the backseat, but because I choose to trust the *with-ness* of God in my life, I select the music on the radio, and fear no longer drives.

> The *with-ness* of the Divine points us to better "what if" questions.

- What if God has a beautiful and perfect plan for my life that is greater than anything I've ever imagined?
- What if this darkness is part of that grand plan unfolding in my life?
- What if something far greater awaits me on the other side of this struggle?
- What if the God who can calm the wind and stop the waves with his words is in my boat?
- What if I choose to trust God with my life—even if he doesn't stop this raging storm?

Do we trust the *with-ness* of the Divine in our lives? Because he is there. He has always been there. Are we willing to trust that? Trust him? When fear is screaming for our attention, will we choose instead to listen to that still, quiet voice that says, "Fear not. I am with you. I am here and I will never leave you?"

God wastes nothing—not even the weeks and months I spent living in fear. I used to believe that fear and faith could not coexist—that I could be one or the other, fearful or faithful—but not both at the same time. God used my experience with cancer to teach me that fear and faith can coexist. I can experience both. But when I chose to focus on my fears and push faith to the side, God felt distant, and I felt like a sojourner out there on my own, feeling the full weight of the darkness in my life, alone and desperate. But when I chose to stand in faith, despite my fear, to trust God with my life, even the possible end of my life, I was surrounded by a peace that comes from the *with-ness* of the Divine. God's *with-ness* puts fear in the backseat, still along for the ride, but no longer in control.

- Have you been living your life consumed by fear?
- Are you tired of waking fearful to face another day?
- Is fear in the driver's seat, making all the decisions and choosing the music?

You don't have to live that way.

You can put fear in the backseat. You can free yourself of fear's control and choose the path to living the firm-grip life where fear doesn't win the battle for your mind. But like my journey, you must shift the way you think about fear. Realize you have far more control over fear than you knew. You can choose hope over fear and you don't have to do it alone. You have the *with-ness* of the Divine, every moment, every breath, every day.

You simply choose to rest in his *with-ness*
because in the firm-grip life,
you are never alone.

10

Keeping Score

Life Marker: Comparison

Confidence isn't walking into a room and thinking you're better than everyone, it's walking in and not having to compare yourself to anyone at all.
—Author unknown

I love books. I love everything about them—the way a book feels in my hands, the smell of the pages, and how they look on a shelf. Primarily, I read nonfiction books about faith and spirituality, personal development, and self-improvement. So many authors I've read are wise and inspire me to live better, love deeper, and know the Divine more fully. When I decided to write this book, I was filled with excitement. I was eager to share my message of hope with others. But my eagerness slowly turned to doubt. How could I possibly write anything as inspiring and hopeful as the authors I've read? Who am I to think I could do what they do? How can my message possibly be as helpful and inspiring as theirs?

I wrote this entire book fighting doubt that I had anything worth sharing.

This is a good place for me to admit that I've always struggled with comparing myself to others. It's a bad habit I work hard at eliminating from my life. As bizarre as this may sound, I even remember comparing myself to people who didn't have cancer. I'd see a person in some everyday setting and think about them not having cancer (at least not to my knowledge anyway). They had something I didn't—a cancer-free body. I was so caught up in playing the comparison game I played even though I knew nothing about that person's health.

I now work very hard to live differently. Every day, I'm intentional about avoiding the trappings of the comparison game, and when I am drawn in, shifting my thoughts from negative thinking.

I think most people spend too much energy comparing themselves to others to see how they stack up. It's an exhausting game and rarely leads to anything healthy or helpful. So let me say this right now—

Choosing to live the firm-grip life
helps us discover our self-worth
without comparing ourselves to others.

Comparison is almost always centered in self-doubt—a belief that something about ourself is lacking, that we're not enough. Just more fear-driven lies we tell ourselves. Social media has elevated the comparison game to a major league level, but since the beginning of time humans have stacked themselves against others to see how they measured up. The comparison game is deeply embedded in the human narrative and began with the very first humans to walk the Earth. And since there were only two of them, they started the game on a much larger scale with God as their point of comparison. To discover the origins of the comparison game, we have to go all the way back to the beginning of creation found in Genesis.

Gardens and Games

After God created the Heavens and Earth, day and night, water and land, plants and animals, he created Adam and Eve in His own image, breathed his own breath into them and they became alive. And God put them in charge of the whole thing. They were king and queen and all the Earth was their kingdom. Genesis 1 was very good for Adam and Eve.

In Genesis 2, God gave them only one rule—don't eat from the tree of knowledge of good and evil. He told them they could eat from any other tree, but this tree, if they ate from it, they would die. Pretty clear, right? And with the consequence of death for violating that rule, it should be easy to stay far away from that tree, right?

Unfortunately, Adam and Eve weren't sure how they measured up, even though they had the very breath of God in their lungs. They wondered if they were good enough. If maybe, even, they should be better.

Along came the serpent in Genesis 3 who asked Eve, "Did God actually say, 'you shall not eat of any tree in the garden'?" Eve told him they could eat from any tree they wanted to—except one—which would kill them.

"Nonsense," said the snake, "God knows that if you eat from that tree, you won't die, but instead your eyes will be opened and you'll be *like God*"—the ultimate comparison statement. Of course, Eve told all of this to Adam.

To be clear, Adam and Eve had the best deal going at the time. The whole Earth and everything in it were theirs. They didn't have to share with anyone. There was no one better than them, no one higher ranking than them, no one with a better thing going than them, no one who had more than them—except one—the One who created them—God himself.

When the snake told them they could be like God, what did they do? They compared themselves to the only Being that was higher than them and they decided they wanted what God had. They wanted more because someone else (God) had something more than they had. So, they made their decision and became the first humans to play the comparison game.

If you know the story, it didn't work out too well for them. But that's not surprising because playing the comparison game typically yields poor results. Kicked out of the garden, Adam and Eve lost their kingdom and felt shame in the presence of their Creator.

So started the game humans play of comparing themselves to each other, looking to see if someone else is better off and how to even the score—or better yet, up the ante.

Who's Winning?

The comparison game is a dominant theme in human life. Humans across all generations play the game every day. Who's better than who? Little kids see their playmate's toy... Older kids look at what their classmates wear to school... Adults see others with better jobs, better looks, a nicer house, more money, newer cars, better-behaved kids, cooler vacations, a greener lawn. On and on we go trying to see how we measure up against others, hoping somehow, we at least are even, or better yet, slightly ahead.

The problem is the game never ends. No matter how many rounds of the game you win, no matter how many points you give yourself, no matter how many players you defeat, there will always be more players, and there will always be someone better.

It's toxic, and it's exhausting.

Culture is designed to perpetuate the comparison game. Every television commercial is an attempt to convince you that your life will be better and YOU will be better if you have what the people in the commercial have. The message humans hear is that we'll be happier people, more important people, more satisfied people if we have more and are more.

Social media drives the game too. People post photos of their best moments. We see our friends on vacation, at the fancy restaurant, in the front row of the big game and we wonder why we can't have their life. And even though we know we're comparing the highlight reel of their life to our ordinary, everyday life, we convince ourselves we simply... don't... stack... up.

Despair and self-doubt often settle in
and take root in our mind,
convincing us we are not enough.

To be clear, I'm not condemning healthy motivation, healthy competition even. In fact, comparing ourselves to others through a healthy perspective can inspire and motivate us to work hard to become better people. But the toxic comparison game I'm talking about isn't grounded in inspiration and motivation—it's grounded in self-condemnation, self-pity, and self-doubt. When we live in those spaces, negative thoughts control our minds and our focus becomes negative—toward everyone and everything. Jealousy and envy often arise, completing the attack on our thoughts.

The Human Response to the Comparison Game

When we play the comparison game, we typically have one of two responses, neither of which are beneficial nor will point us to living the firm-grip life. The first response we may experience is failure. We compare ourselves, decide we don't measure up, and we allow feelings of inferiority to attack us. We question our self-worth. We need to accomplish more, have more, do more, be more… to have value.

The other response is self-righteousness, the belief we're better than the other player. This response, like the game itself, has deep roots in the history of mankind, as illustrated in the parable in Luke 18. Here, the players are two people from opposite ends of the social scale.

> "Two men went up to the temple to pray, one a Pharisee and the other a tax collector. The Pharisee stood by himself and prayed: 'God, I thank you that I am not like other people—robbers, evildoers, adulterers—or even like this tax collector. I fast twice a week and give a tenth of all I get.'" Luke 18: 10-12 (NIV)

The Pharisee awarded himself more points than the tax collector. He was better. He won the game, declared himself the victor, and cast judgment and condemnation on the other player to assure he stood out as superior (in his own mind). When we judge others as inferior, less than, it's only because we played the game, compared ourselves to that person, self-appointed ourselves as judge, and decided we are the better person, the winner of that round.

Doesn't sound very kind when I put it that way, does it? Yet it's our reality if we're honest. Think of the last time you walked past a homeless person on the streets. Sure, you may have felt pity, maybe even dropped five dollars in the cup, but at some level, didn't you compare and play the game? Maybe it was the simple thought of, "I'm thankful I'm not him." That's exactly what the Pharisee said. See the danger now? We're so ingrained in the game, it feels natural, normal, justified even to compare, compete, and keep score.

So how do we stop playing the comparison game?

We don't.
Wait, what?

I don't think it's possible to stop comparing ourselves to others. It's too deeply ingrained in the human experience for the game to stop. But we can learn to play the game in ways that lead us to healthy thoughts and a positive focus on our lives.

Shifts and Choices

Jesus continues the parable in the book of Luke.

"But the tax collector stood at a distance. He would not
even look up to Heaven, but beat his breast and said, 'God
have mercy on me a sinner.'" Luke 18: 13 (NIV)

It would be easy to presume the tax collector decided he wasn't playing the game, that he took the higher road. Or we could conclude the tax collector didn't see the Pharisee in the temple so he wasn't in the game at all. History would tell us otherwise, for in those times, people who went to the temple said their prayers aloud, for all to hear. The words of the Pharisee undoubtedly rang in the ears of the tax collector as a stinging reminder of the tax collector's lesser social status within the Jewish culture. Not only was the tax collector rudely invited into the comparison game, but his opponent proudly proclaimed the tax collector as the loser for all to hear.

So how can we understand the tax collector's attitude in the temple when he was just called out in front of everyone in the temple? Jesus finished the parable.

"I tell you that this man, rather than the other, went home
justified before God. For all those who exalt themselves
will be humbled and those who humble themselves will be
exalted." Luke 18: 14 (NIV)

The tax collector, although undoubtedly in the game, shifted his focus off the Pharisee and onto himself. He had no interest in trying to determine how he measured up against the Pharisee. He didn't see himself as inferior to the Pharisee, nor did he see himself as better. Instead, he humbled himself, looked at his own life, and responded out of humility. He didn't care how he stacked up in his relationship to the Pharisee—he was only concerned about his relationship to the God who created him to be him, not who someone else defined him to be.

So how do you live like the tax collector?

First, shift the way you think. Instead of trying to determine how you measure up against others, focus on who God made you to be. Remind yourself you are created in the image of the God of the universe, the Creator of all things, the One whose very breath is in your lungs. Realize God made you uniquely you. You are not like anyone else and no one else is like you. This world desperately needs you to be the person God created you to be. You have an incredible contribution to make to this world... as you... when you align your heart's desire with becoming exactly who God created you to be. You don't have to feel compelled to denigrate yourself or judge others because you trust your Creator's vision for who you are to be. You can shift your thoughts to the truth that God designed you to be uniquely special so you can choose to focus on being you.

How liberating!

Second, live with conscientious intentionality. Remain aware of your thoughts. When you know your thoughts have drifted into comparing yourself to another person, act with intentionality to redirect your thoughts from the other person and back to you, what you have, the blessings in your life, and who you are at a core, values-based level. The best way to do this is to focus on gratitude. If you've developed a consistent, daily practice of gratitude as we discussed in chapter eight, that core gratitude gesture of your soul will help you redirect your thoughts toward positive thinking patterns that will free you from the pitfalls of comparison.

Third, the next time you find yourself tempted to respond out of jealousy and envy when the other player in the game seems to have more than you or appears better than you, take a moment to express happiness over their good fortune. Yes. Be happy for them. It's amazing how expressing pleasure for another person's accomplishments will re-adjust your attitude toward both the other person and you.

Finally, remind yourself daily that you make your own choices. You have full control over how you respond when you find yourself in the game, comparing yourself to another person. Remaining aware of your choices will help keep you from lapsing into default response patterns of negative thinking.

One of the unexpected gifts that cancer brought into my life was a new appreciation for who God created me to be. Somehow, all these crazy twists and turns my life has taken, including this journey with cancer, are part of who I am, and part of who I am created to be. There was a time, in my darkest moments, I'd have traded my life with anyone. I'd have done almost anything to be someone else, have someone else's path, live someone else's life, anything to avoid my dance with this devil.

I don't think that way anymore. The firm-grip life has helped me shift my thoughts and make new choices. Even if this evil ravages my body someday, I want to be me because I trust that God created me with his intent and his purpose and that's where I want to live. Sure, I still get sucked into the comparison game. I'm human and we humans will probably always play this game. But I can enter the arena with great confidence because I know who I am. And as long as my heart's desire remains aligned with God's intention for my life, I'm perfectly satisfied with being me, cancer and all.

Those who have endured the dark sometimes see life differently than others—to our advantage. We now care less about what others have and are more grateful for what we have. We can play the comparison game and often see that it reveals the beauty of our own lives more than reflects the perceptions of others' lives. New perspectives often create contentment and peace we didn't previously experience, allowing us to express more gratitude for what we have and who we are.

You survived your darkness.
You're still here.
God's breath is in your lungs.
There's no one like you.

Remember that the next time you play the game.

11

A Different Kind of Cancer

Life Marker: Complaining

You can never complain your way to a fulfilling life.
—Edmond Mbiaka

The thing about cancer is we don't know it's there—until we know it's there. Some cancers grow quickly while others take time to twist their way into your body and life. Cancer starts with a cell mutation. Our bodies have millions of cells. Every day, some cells mutate, for reasons not always known. Most of the time our natural body systems do what they're designed to do and correct the mutation, or prevent the mutation from creating damage. This might occur several thousand times a day. Our bodies know what is and isn't allowed to occur and it corrects itself, like the autocorrect feature on your cell phone or tablet.

Once in a while a mutated cell escapes detection and slips through the cracks. Now undetected, that cell may mutate again… and again… and again, hundreds, thousands of times. Like a dog left at home alone, it creates its own mischief. At the end of its run of misbehavior, those mutations result in the first cancerous cell.

At that moment, that person has cancer—he or she just doesn't know it yet.

I couldn't help but wonder how long I had cancer before my diagnosis. I asked the doctor who discovered the lump in my throat and the surgeon who removed it. Both refused to guess, but both were confident it had been hitching a ride in my neck for quite some time, maybe years. During its habitation, the cancer expanded, branched out, and explored its neighborhood. The only confirmed visits it made were to the two lymph nodes in my neck discovered in post-surgical pathology.

There's not much certainty with cancer. But one thing that is typically certain is the cancer had been there for a while, growing, wreaking havoc, and slowly causing damage in its host before it was discovered.

Slowly but Surely

Like cancer, there are other things that take time to create damage in our lives. Unlike a car crash that causes sudden, instant injury and damage, the choices we make daily can create slow, subtle damage that builds over the years until one day we notice the destructive results. Often, we don't recognize the damage is even building. Many times, the first clue is the onset of mass chaos in our lives that changes everything. Sure, maybe we knew there was a "little problem" but never did we imagine how that problem would fester into a destructive force in our lives. Let me give you a couple of examples.

I have a friend who enjoyed a cold beer, a glass of wine, or a cocktail once in a while. He started drinking in college. After college, he began a career, got married, and had children. Soon the stresses of life arrived, as they always do. To take the edge off, my friend began to drink liquor every day. He said the drinks helped him relax. A few years later, he needed that drink to start the day, to get his mind clear. It wasn't long before workday lunches included a few drinks to help get him through the afternoon.

Over twenty years, his alcohol consumption increased to the point that he felt better intoxicated than sober. Then the wheels fell off. His drinking affected his work performance, and he lost his job. His wife threatened to leave if he didn't deal with his drinking problem. After years of treatment, my friend slowly found his way to sobriety. Along the way, he suffered a lot of collateral damage, some of which is permanent. My friend didn't wake one day and decide to become an alcoholic. But over the years, like a cancer, excessive drinking slowly crafted its damage in his life.

Sadly, over the years I've had several friends whose marriages ended in divorce. Every one of those divorces surprised me. From my vantage point, they appeared happily married. As I talked with them, however, they all revealed similar stories. Each shared small problems that began years prior. Each said they just assumed the problems would resolve on their own, that addressing the problems seemed more difficult than the problems themselves and they never imagined the unresolved problems would lead to divorce. Little did these friends realize their unaddressed marital problems were slowly eroding the relationship, that over time there was a building resentment within their marriage that was gradually destroying the bond, and that the long-term damage would result in divorce.

Toxic Conversation

It may seem odd, but complaining has much in common with the growth of my cancer, my friend's problem with alcohol, and the end of several friends' marriages.

Complaining may seem rather harmless at first, even invisible, but over time its negative effects build and create long-term damage in our lives. Complaining creates a negative mindset that left unharnessed, grows into a destructive force, turning us bitter and negative. Here's a challenge—

Try to remember one time you complained about
something
then felt inspired, uplifted, and positive.

Have you ever been around a chronic complainer? They complain about everything. Rarely do they have anything good or positive to say about anyone or anything. For them, life has become dark and negative, their thoughts jaded and cynical. After a conversation with a chronic complainer, we usually feel drained, negative, and depressed. Sometimes we don't even know why we feel that way. We have become accustomed to complaint-driven conversations that leave us unable to even identify the negative effects in our lives.

Complaining is destructive for both the complainer and the listener. The complainer creates a negative environment that turns both conversation participants negative. In many situations, the complainer draws in the listener and the listener joins in complaining, both parties commiserating together, feeding off each other's negativity. Often that's just what the complainer desires—to draw the listener in and engage the listener in a negative dialogue so the listener validates their complaints.

> Birthed from negativity,
> complaining perpetuates more negativity
> and over time,
> creates a negative life narrative.
> The firm-grip life can help us eliminate (or at least reduce)
> complaining.

What Are You Complaining About?

Despite the destructive consequences of complaining, most of us are pretty good at it. Humans complain about everything—the weather, traffic, our significant other, work, politics, our favorite sports team, and our kids. We complain if the coffee is too cold or too hot. We complain when our flight is delayed. We complain when we wait too long at the doctor's office. We complain that our homes are too small and our bellies too big. We complain about potholes in the street and road construction that fixes the potholes. We complain the sermon was too long and the vacation too short. We complain... and we complain... and we complain. Despite all the good in our lives, our conversations usually focus on our complaints. We complain so much that we don't even realize we're complaining. Complaining has become part of our normal, daily conversations, a default method of interacting with others.

> And most of the time,
> we

aren't

even

aware

of

it.

Like a sneeze during flu season, every time we complain, we spew negativity all over ourselves and the unfortunate recipient of our verbal venom. Complaining creates stress, for both the complainer and the listener which raises our cortisol level, a natural hormone released when we're stressed. Raised cortisol levels contribute to a suppressed immune system, hypertension, high blood sugar, type 2 diabetes, and fat storage. Stress negatively impacts our circulation, raises our blood pressure, and increases risk for heart disease and cancer. If the physical health detriments are not bad enough, stress shifts our brain into habitual patterns of negative thinking that can lead to unhealthy relationships, depression, anger, and mental illness.

What's worse, complaining rarely does anything to change the situation we're complaining about. When did your complaints about your boss ever result in your boss behaving differently? Most likely, all your complaints did was upset you more and create more hostility toward your boss, making your work environment worse than before you started complaining. Complaining about my cancer would have done nothing to cure me but would have only made a difficult circumstance more challenging by creating more negative thoughts.

Complaining about circumstances over which we have no control or are unwilling to exercise control is futile and will never point us toward a positive life narrative. In fact, the opposite is true; complaining will only create a negative life narrative.

So how do we change lifelong habits of complaining?

How do we curtail our complaining when we seldom even recognize its existence in our conversations?

And how do we avoid the negative impact as the recipient of other's complaints?

The No-Complaining Zone

Until I was aware I had a cancerous tumor, there was nothing I could do to take action to remove it and its negative impact on my body. It was only through becoming aware of its presence that I could take action to deal with the problem. The same principle applies to eradicating complaining from your life.

You must become aware of its presence in your conversations.

That requires intentionality.

You have to be mindful of your conversations at work, during lunch with friends, at home with your family, and even in meetings at church. You have to develop the practice of listening to your own words, paying attention to the conversations you have and what flows out of your mouth. This is easiest accomplished if you start with a small goal.

Commit yourself to one hour of no complaining.

One.

Single.

Hour.

Pick one hour to intentionally guard yourself against complaining. Commit to being mindful of each conversation. When you catch yourself complaining, don't consider it a failure, consider it a success that you recognized that you complained. That awareness will foster more awareness. Then try another hour. See if you can string a few hours together. Each hour will bring a growing awareness of your conversations. Each hour will result in fewer and fewer complaints and with that success will come reduced negative thinking.

Then an amazing thing happens: As you reduce your negative thoughts, there's more space for positive thoughts. This gives you the opportunity to reflect on your complaining and choose a better path.

When you find yourself about to complain about something, ask yourself if the issue will still be a problem next month, next week, tomorrow, or even an hour from now. Often the issues we complain about are fleeting in time, soon to be irrelevant. If the issue isn't there for the long haul, let it go—it's not worth your time or energy to complain about it.

Before verbalizing any complaint, ask yourself if you're willing to take action to rectify the issue. Are you willing to be a part of the solution? If not, choose to hold back your complaint. If the issue isn't worthy of your time and energy to resolve, it's not worthy of your time and energy to complain about it.

There are times however when you may have a righteous complaint, a legitimate reason to be upset. When you see a true injustice, it's natural, proper even to bring that injustice to light, to expose a wrong. But in doing so, prepare to be a part of the solution, not just expose the problem. When you are part of solving a problem, rather than just complaining about the problem, you experience positive effects on your thought life rather than negative consequences—not to mention the effect you can have on the situation itself.

If you need to vent, to let out built-up frustrations, find a trusted friend you can talk to. Repressing tension is unhealthy, but finding a positive outlet is essential. Share your concerns but then ask your friend to help you work through the issue, to find healthy ways to address the problem so you can move forward without the continuing negativity created by the problem. Start the conversation by telling your friend you need support as opposed to launching into a complaint. But be careful not to seek validation of your frustration over seeking a solution to the problem. And understand there may not always be a solution, that the best solution sometimes is simply talking through the issue with a wise friend.

When others complain to you, offer solutions rather than consolation. Bring attention to any positives identified in the situation. There are always positives—it's simply a choice to see them. The quickest way to diffuse a complaint is to turn the complaint into an opportunity to improve the situation. Point your friend to the possible solutions rather than validating the complaint.

The most effective method to prevent ourselves from complaining is to shift our focus to gratitude, the foundational bass note of the firm-grip life. It's difficult to complain when our focus is on gratitude. I can easily fall into the trap of complaining, but when gratitude is in my heart, it's difficult to have complaints on my tongue. They simply can't coexist within the same mindset. So, it's a choice—one or the other. When I catch myself complaining, naming something I am grateful for is a great way to follow up a complaint. When I follow a complaint with gratitude, I'm able to sever the flow of negative energy and thoughts and immediately shift back to my firm-grip life.

One Hour to Firm-Grip Living

Complaining is a choice. Not complaining is a choice. Once again, we find ourselves with a choice, a choice which either points us toward a negative life narrative, or a positive life narrative.

Choosing to complain is easy.

Wisdom calls us to so much more, something much greater. Wisdom calls us to new ways of thinking, new ways of being in the world, new ways to respond to what life throws our way. Wisdom calls us to a place of peace that allows us to accept things as they are, to seek the good in all things, and to live with gratitude. This better way of being human doesn't make all our problems disappear, rather this new way of thinking and choosing helps us intentionally create a future that is positive-focused and will radically alter the trajectory of our life.

When you choose the firm-grip life and become aware of the words you speak and begin to eliminate complaining from your life, your life will shift toward positive-focused living. Only then will you truly realize the negative impact complaining has on your mindset and your life. It will take time and it will take consistent intentionality to make this shift in the way you think and the choices you make.

So, start small.

Pick an hour and start today.

12

Running Through Brick Walls

Life Marker: Chasing Approval

The unhappiest people in this world are those who care the most about what others think.
—C. Joy Bell C.

I remember the last baseball game I ever played. I was an eighteen-year-old high school senior. Our team was eliminated from the state tournament. Our season was over. For many of us, our baseball careers were done. We'd never play another game other than the occasional pickup game at a family reunion—but it's not a real baseball game when you have to give your Aunt four strikes before she's out.

I remember sitting in the dugout after that game, processing the reality of never again putting on a baseball uniform, never again stepping onto a field with the smell of fresh-cut grass, never again hopping over the newly laid chalk line on the way to my second base position. There would be no more double plays, no more late-inning comebacks, and I would never again utter the words, "Hey batter, batter."

It was a great season, but one cut short by our surprising, early departure from the tournament. To his credit, Coach Schreiber did his best to soothe the pain of the loss by reminding us of the successful season. He also talked about each player who had reached the end of his last season in the game.

I was just an average player on my best days so Coach had to dig a little deeper to find words to speak about me. But I remember them well. He said, "There was always one thing I could count on about Nelly (his nickname for me); if I asked Nelly to run through a brick wall, he'd die trying." I realize Coach meant that statement as a compliment to my commitment to give my all on every play, every day. But as I look back on that statement decades later, I realize there was more lurking in that statement that would define parts of my life in the years that followed.

While I was no doubt dedicated to giving my best effort, there was something more driving me—I wanted Coach's approval. I wanted him to respect me. I wanted him to think highly of me. I wanted him to like me. I wanted to please him. My need for his favorable opinion of me drove me as much as my desire to perform well, maybe more so.

While there is nothing bad about any of those motivations, when those motivations of pleasing others to gain their approval become a driving factor in our lives, we set ourselves up for a very difficult life, often full of disappointment and dissatisfaction. That day may have been the end of my baseball career, but it was just the beginning of my career as a people pleaser, a seeker of other's favorable opinions of me, a career I pursued for years.

Cool Kids

It starts when we're kids. We walk into the classroom on our first day of school and with very little social experience under our belts, we quickly figure out who the cool kids are. More importantly, we know right away that we want to be one of the cool kids because it's clear that everyone likes the cool kids. The cool kids have the best clothes and the coolest backpacks. The cool kids hang out together, a self-appointed elite group that quickly separates itself from the other kids. On the playground, the cool kids decide who gets to play with them and who doesn't. The cool kids sit together at the same lunch table and in the same section on the school bus. They know they're the cool kids. And the rest of the kids? —they know they're not.

Longing to be one of the cool kids, the uncool kids embark on a journey of wanting to fit in, to be recognized, to be liked, striving to be a cool kid. The typical result is doing things, saying things, and acting in certain ways to please the cool kids, gain their approval and maybe get an invitation to be a cool kid.

Life doesn't change much as we age, does it? The desire to be accepted, liked, respected, and admired continues into adult life. We want to fit in, belong to the group. At times we go to great lengths in our effort to please others, impress them, prove we're worthy of their approval and high opinions. Some people pursue a career in a field they believe will earn them the respect and acceptance of their peers. Others buy expensive houses in the "right neighborhood" or purchase expensive, luxury cars in hopes others will grant their approval as a declaration that "you fit in." Pursuing followers and "likes" on social media is the way some aim to please others hoping to earn their respect and acceptance.

We pursue all of this because we have this instinctive need for acceptance, to fit in, to know we belong. While it's normal to desire to fit in, far too often, we conform our conduct solely to please others to earn their favorable opinions as to the means by which we measure our value. Or said another way, we allow our perception of others' opinions of us to determine how we live, how we conduct ourselves, and how we determine our self-worth.

But here's a hard but important truth: It's impossible to live the firm-grip life when we live to please others and allow other people's opinions to define our self-worth.

Living for the approval of others becomes a full-time job. Every time we step out of our home and into the world, every interaction with another person, every word we speak gets filtered through our concern of whether someone else will think we're enough, whether we're worthy of their acceptance, whether we'll get to be a cool kid.

Who Will I be Today?

Over my lifetime, I've struggled with insecurity and the desire to fit in, to be accepted. I'm sure a psychologist would enjoy digging deep into my psyche to determine the cause of that struggle whether it be low self-esteem, lack of confidence, or some other deep-rooted cause that traces back to some early childhood trauma. Whatever the cause, I recall the stress of entering new social settings and the anxiety of wondering how I would fit in. More so, I remember the angst of wondering what I needed to do, how I needed to act or what I needed to say to please the people in that group in hopes they would like me and accept me.

> I was driven by their opinion of me.
> I was driven by who I thought I needed to be.

Typically, I'd figure it out and conform my conduct to gain acceptance. But over time, a problem arose: I engaged more and more groups of people—work, church, friends, clubs and associations and other social groups. Each group was different, each seeming to have their own form of secret handshake. Shameful as it feels now, I became a chameleon, changing who I needed to be to fit the group I was with. As a result, I invented many versions of myself, false selves, each one serving my perceived expectations of the group I was with at the moment. Convinced I was not enough, rarely did I allow myself to live out of my true, authentic self.

I believe the greatest threat from living a life aimed at pleasing others to gain favorable opinions is that we lose track of who we are. We adapt who we are and become someone(s) we're not. This way of living is an exhausting energy drain. We live in a constant state of identity crisis. When we go to work, we become our work self and act and talk in whatever manner is expected to fit in at work. When we play in the golf or softball league, we become yet another person, trying to fit in on the team. On Sunday, they require the church self, as few of our other created identities will fit well there. Sometimes, we even create a false self that takes over around family, who we often perceive have their own unique expectations.

We create so many false selves that there remains little room for who we really are, our one true self. For many, this is the cyclical pattern of life, day after day, month after month, year after year—for their entire life. The true self gets suppressed somewhere deep, maybe so deep that it's barely even recognizable anymore, even to ourselves. I suspect many people die having suppressed their true selves to the end. They could never free themselves from the relentless pursuit of pleasing others.

> There is little more tragic than living a lifetime and never being you.

Created to Be Me

- If you knew you were dying, would other's opinions of you still matter?
- Would you continue to live out of false selves to please or impress others?
- Would you still care to be one of the cool kids?

Well, I have to tell you something: I'm dying. That may come as a bit of a surprise based on earlier chapters, but it's true. I'm getting closer to the end of my life. Each day that passes is one day closer to my death. Today, I have one less day to live than I had yesterday. That said, I don't know when my day will come. I don't know if cancer will take me out, and if it does, I don't know if that will be soon or later. But I know there will come a day that is my last day. And every moment I'm alive brings my end closer.

As you might expect, my cancer journey caused me to re-think a lot. The five months between diagnosis and that all-important first round of post-operative blood tests was one of the most challenging periods I've ever lived through, yet the most rewarding as well (much easier observed now than in the middle of it). I spent five months not knowing if I was living or dying, and if I was dying, how soon that would happen. During some of those days, I found inexplainable courage. Other days, courage didn't seem to exist anywhere in this galaxy. But one thing was consistent—I thought much about how I wanted to live my life going forward, for however many days, months or years remained.

Priorities quickly realign when one of your possible realities is a departure from this life, earlier than expected. Rising to the near top of my list was a new commitment to be me, to live out of who my Creator designed me to be, to live each day as my true, authentic self. Honestly, I wasn't even sure what that meant or looked like. My five months of self-reflection revealed far too many false selves on the resume of my life.

I wasn't even sure I knew how to live as me.

But I knew I was going to or die trying (pun intended).

As I embarked on this new effort to live out of my true self—the real me with a conscience and deep convictions, foundational beliefs, and a moral compass all designed by my Creator—I soon learned this was a frightening proposition. I knew the number of people I'd allowed to see the real me was small. Shelving the fake versions of me, I had to walk into every environment as one person—me. What would people think? How would they react? Would they withdraw their approval of me, disrupt my feelings of acceptance? Would I fit in anywhere anymore? Would they like the real me?

Of course, these questions led me right back to the start of how I got to this place, to begin with—wanting to be liked, accepted, and approved—a cool kid. So, I had to disregard these questions completely and the thoughts that created them.

I had to find the courage
to live out of my true self,
regardless of how others responded.

Needing a source of inspiration and courage to live like me, I turned to the wisdom traditions found in the ancient scriptures of Proverbs where I discovered this verse:

"The fear of human opinions disables; trusting in God protects you from that." Proverbs 29:25 (The Message)

This passage reminded me of a spiritual truth I'd known for decades but had suppressed along with my true self: A perfect Creator created me with Divinely selected uniqueness according to his plan for my life and his intention for my contributions to this world. The Divine had already accepted me, as he created me, and with all the flaws I constructed and added to the mix of who I am.

Despite the drive of humans to seek approval from others,
every one of us is
approved,
accepted,
embraced,
welcomed,
and loved
by the Creator of the universe!
Just as we are.

Armed with my new resolve, a faith-fueled passion, and a commitment to live the firm-grip life, I began to live as me, some days more boldly than others and some days defaulting to a well-known, safe, more predictable false version of me. But slowly, over time, and with increasing courage, I lived more and more as the real me.

I'll admit it has not been an easy process, nor has it come without discomfort. As one might suspect, not everyone embraced the real me. But in fairness, I had never let most see the real me before, only a false version. I now realize how unfair that was—I never gave others the chance to accept the real me, acting under my preconceived notion that I was not enough.

Possibly my greatest learning from shedding my false selves has been the realization that living out of my true self has created a much more positive focus in my life. I did not fully appreciate the negative effects on my attitude caused by living through a false self. By liberating myself to live as me, I noticed an increase in positive thinking patterns. As I gained confidence in my commitment to live as me, previously unnoticed burdens lifted from my mind. My eyes opened to the stress and anxiety suddenly absent from my life. I felt indescribably free—still vulnerable, but free.

Created to Be You

I've got more news for you. You're dying too. At the end of this day on which you're reading this sentence, you will have one less day to live, you will be one day closer to your death. Sorry. But it's your reality. You have some number of days left—it's the number that's uncertain. Faced with that reality, I decided I had no other choice than to live as the real me.

What about you?

I realize what I'm asking you to consider is frightening, terrifying even. But the invitation is to liberate yourself from a prison in which you may not have even realized you were living, a prison that has likely created significant negativity in your life, even if you didn't know it. But you're not alone. God has promised to protect you if you place your trust in him.

> Choosing to live the firm-grip life
> will energize you with the confidence you need
> to simply... be... you.

You no longer have to try to run through brick walls to please others and chase their favorable opinions. And in this place of freedom, you will find peace and contentment as promised in the book of Matthew:

> "You're blessed when you're content with just who you
> are—no more, no less. That's the moment you find
> yourselves proud owners of everything that can't be
> bought." Matthew 5:4-5 (The Message)

The firm-grip life is a declaration that we are not other's opinions of us. It's an intentional way of living that embraces who we were created to be. I believe you have a yearning from deep within to live out of your true self as the person the Divine created you to be. I believe there is a longing in you that desires to shed your false selves and embrace your own truth, an instinct carefully crafted into you by your Creator.

So, where does your journey start? It starts where most of the ideas in this book start—with a shift in the way you think and the decision to make new choices. A shift from believing your self-worth is found in the opinions and pleasures of others to a new understanding that your Divine Creator has already accepted you as you are, created with a Divine plan and purpose. A shift from believing you have to conform to please others to an understanding that living out of your authentic self will allow you to make your greatest contribution to the world. Maybe your first shift requires that you recognize that you don't have to conform to be accepted by God—that God already thinks quite highly of you.

With these new understandings comes the opportunity to make new choices—choices to trust that your best version of you is the true version of you, the version created with great intentionality by a God who accepts and loves you. Choices to live courageously from your real self, to create more positive-focused living by being who God created you to be. Choices to offer your greatest contribution to the world from your own uniqueness.

The world desperately needs you to be you.
But just as importantly, you desperately need you to be
you.

Choosing to live the firm-grip life will help you begin the journey to rediscover who you are at your deepest core and give you the courage to live intentionally, passionately, and unapologetically from that person.

Darkness shines more light than we realize. What you've been through—what I've been through—often points us to new understandings of ourselves. Allow your journey to point you within—to the beautiful, one and only you, created perfectly in the image of your Divine Creator and free the real you from the trappings of a life trying to run through brick walls to please others. Not only will you be free, but the world will see the real you.

And that's exactly what the world needs right now.

13

When Less is More

Life Marker: Stuff

Wanting less is a better blessing than having more.
—Mary Ellen Edmunds

Several years ago, I visited the country of Haiti with a group from our church. The trip was a medical trip. The traveling group included doctors, nurses, and a dentist who traveled to Haiti often to provide free medical care to people living in or near Jacmel. Others joined the group to provide support for the medical professionals and interact with the people who came to the clinics.

Our church established a presence in Haiti many years before this trip. Through generous donations, we constructed a building in Jacmel that housed a church, feeding center, orphanage, and school. A Haitian pastor led the church and these ministries.

My purpose for tagging along on the trip was different. The deed to the land on which the building sat contained legal flaws, and if the local pastor died, the real estate could become the property of the Haitian government and the services offered to the community would be in jeopardy. My task was to meet with the local judge who, under Haitian law, was the only person who could assist with correcting this problem. This was my first experience with international law in a third-world country. I soon discovered that in a country steeped in massive poverty, money, not law or eloquently presented legal arguments, controls the results. After a few days of negotiations, we successfully resolved the issue and were assured (as much as anything is sure in a third-world country) that the ministries could continue well into the future.

Aside from my interactions with the Haitian legal system, I was shocked at the level of poverty I witnessed—devastating poverty. I'd seen pictures and others tried to warn me, but nothing prepared me for what I experienced. From the plane on our final approach into the airport at Port Au Prince, I saw the brownish-colored water in the harbor. A mission trip veteran seated next to me told me that was runoff of sewage into the ocean—confirmed by the stench of raw sewage when we de-boarded the plane. With no modern sewer infrastructure in the country, Haitians have no option but to use the surrounding rivers, ditches, and waterways as a toilet, all of which flows toward the ocean.

Electricity is scarce and is unreliable. With no artificial light, the night sky was the deepest shade of indigo I've ever seen. Oh, how the stars shine with splendor when left to their natural environment without human interference!

Housing reveals a deeper level of despair. There is no running water, only hand-pumped water wells to supply household needs. Entire extended families live in concrete block, one-room structures, most of which are slightly larger than a backyard shed found in American suburbia. Everyone sleeps on the floor of this home that has no bathroom, no kitchen, no bedrooms, and no utilities. One room, nothing more.

Everything I've described is only 838 miles from Florida, a one-and-a-half-hour flight from Miami.

Despite these inhumane living conditions, there was something I observed that was beautiful, mysterious, and painful all at the same time. Most Haitians I met were full of joy. Smiles filled their faces. Kindness lived in their eyes. Love spilled from their hearts. The despair I felt in looking at their living conditions miraculously hadn't transcended their souls. By modern standards, their living conditions pointed to hopelessness, yet they were full of hope. I struggled to understand this.

How could they be so full of joy?
Didn't they know how bad their lives were?
Couldn't they see tomorrow would be no better?

During my five-day stay in Jacmel person after person thanked us. They were grateful for the medical services and basic personal items—toothbrushes, toiletries, T-shirts, and underwear. The children loved to play games, so we spent hours with them. The adults simply appreciated the opportunity to have conversations and practice their English. Over and over, I met joy-filled Haitians, peaceful and content. I couldn't reconcile how any of them could live so content. Yet they were, defying my culture's logic.

Jack and Erik

I met a man named Jack on a scorching afternoon. Jack scooted into the make-shift medical clinic. Although Jack had legs, they were useless. Gnarled and deformed, Jack's feet pointed in unnatural directions. Instead of walking, Jack used his hands to scoot his body. Both of his hands were well-worn and callused. Immediately I knew what was wrong with Jack's feet.

I'd seen feet like those before—in my own home.

My son, Erik, was born with severely disfigured, bilateral club feet, grotesquely twisted, hardly resembling human feet. One foot twisted to a ninety-degree angle. The other, far worse, pointed backward. The agony of the obvious defect threatened the joy of his birth. *Will he ever walk?* was my first thought. Fortunately, Erik was born in America where we had medical insurance and access to the world's best physicians. After a couple of years of treatments and surgeries, Erik's feet were straight and he not only walked, he ran. He's lived a normal life and even played baseball at the collegiate level.

It was more than I could handle when Jack scooted into the clinic. All I could envision was Erik, had he been born in Haiti instead of our land of privilege. Tears flowed. I had to leave the room, find a space where I could gather myself because I knew I had to meet Jack and I needed to compose myself.

Jack greeted me with a smile that lit his eyes as he hugged me. He told me had no family and both his parents died when he was a child. He lived here and there, often sleeping in the streets. He begged for most of his meals and couldn't hold a job. He relied heavily on the ministries of the local church for his daily needs. The only clothes he owned were those he wore, his only possessions those he dragged

behind him in a small bag. I shared Erik's story with him. I told him of his surgeries and how he now walks and runs. He asked to see a picture of Erik. Jack looked at the picture, smiled at me, and said, "God bless him and God bless you."

After that Jack handed me a dirty rag to wipe my leaking eyes.

To my wonder and awe, Jack didn't have a chip on his shoulder. Though he owned nothing, and despite his severely limiting disability, he wasn't angry, nor did he live in despair. He wasn't depressed. He wasn't hopeless. He wasn't negative. Jack found a way, against all odds, to live with a positive attitude toward his life.

During my conversations with Jack and many of the other Haitians, I often asked if they dreamed of living in America. Every answer was the same—no. When I asked why, the oft-repeated reply was, "Why would I want to live in America? I have everything I need right here." Perplexed with that response I pressed further and asked them to explain. Over and over came this response: "I have my family, my friends, and my God. What else do I need?"

I came home from Haiti renewed in spirit yet wrecked emotionally. I arrived home late at night; my wife already asleep. I was glad she was sleeping as I didn't have the emotional strength to talk about the trip yet. The next morning after a hot shower, I buttoned my freshly pressed white shirt, slipped a pair of cuff links into the French cuffs, and put on my impeccably fitted suit coat. As I tied my leather-soled, wing-tip shoes, I struggled. I knew the cost of the clothes on my body was far more than my new Haitian friends would earn in a year. I broke down, ashamed of my excess, yet grateful for the ability, maybe for the first time in my life, to understand the full extent of my excess. I swore I'd never be the same. I swore I'd never again take my blessed life for granted. I swore I'd live differently, and like my new

Haitian friends, fully embrace all I truly need—family, friends, and God.

Time went on.
I forgot.

No, I didn't forget Haiti.
I didn't forget Jack or the others.
But I *forgot*.

There's no clearer way to say that, but I suspect you understand exactly what I mean.

Never Enough

Several years ago, the *Los Angeles Times* reported that the average American household contains 300,000 items.[1] I'll say that a bit slower; three… hundred… thousand… items! Let's pause for a moment to allow that to sink in because it takes some time. You may think you are different but look around the room you're in now, if you're at home. How many items of clothing, cooking utensils, books, or other items are there?

- How did we get to this point of excess?
- How did we become people with so much stuff?
- Maybe the better question is how much stuff do we really need?

I remember visiting my grandmother when I was a child. She lived in a home built in the late 1800s. The rooms were small, the closets tiny, and there was little storage space. There was only one bathroom. The kitchen was small but served its purpose. There was no den, exercise room, media room, laundry room, man cave, or any space dedicated to leisure.

A century later we've mastered the art of building homes that look like the Taj Mahal compared to my grandmother's home. Many now live in homes with walk-in closets larger than the bedrooms in my grandmother's house. We now build rooms dedicated to every purpose imaginable, including separate spaces for kid leisure and adult leisure. Square footage of modern homes has, on average, almost tripled in the last one hundred years. And of course, we filled all these larger spaces with stuff. Apparently about 300,000 items of stuff.

When we became two-car families, we built garages for our cars. Over time, we crammed our garages so full of stuff that many homes now have a three-car garage. Still not large enough, it's common to see cars parked in driveways, the three-car garage so full the cars don't fit. Our consumer-minded solution? Build storage facilities where we can store the stuff we're not using.

Yeah, those last five words got my attention too: *the stuff we're not using.*

We might need those items again, right? Someday? Maybe? Well, until we find a use for all those items, Americans will continue to pay over $38 billion dollars per year to store them in storage units across America.

How Did We Get Here?

Back to my question: How did we get to this point of excess? There are likely as many reasons as there are items in our homes, but there are some recurring themes that drive us to own so many possessions:

- The desire for status.
- The perceived need to keep up with trends, particularly in fashion.
- We played the comparison game and fell short.
- Belief that the newest, coolest stuff will bring us acceptance and approval from others.
- An overreliance on convenience.
- The reflex that if something is available it is necessary.
- Belief that we'll be happy if we just have _____ (insert name of shiny new item).

Regardless of the reasons for your excess, I'm confident you agree that the amassing of your possessions has likely not fulfilled the reasons you acquired them. Just as you likely didn't recognize that impressing others was driving your purchases, the friends you wanted to impress probably didn't even notice. The happiness you sought lasted a day, maybe only a few hours. The trends you were keeping up with changed the next season. If we're honest, and take a long look at our stuff, much of it has only brought grief and misery to our lives. The more stuff we have the more time we spend cleaning, fixing, organizing, and rearranging to make room for more.

Did you really enjoy pulling all that stuff out to clean the garage, only to pile it all back in, all the while wondering when the last time was you used half of it? What about all those closets jammed with stuff you've been trying to find time to organize for the past year? How many items of clothing hang in your closet or fill your dresser drawers that you no longer like, don't fit (but might someday), or you forgot are even there? Do you even dare go into the basement or attic? Or does the thought of those piles cause too much stress?

The stress doesn't stay at home with our stuff. It follows us everywhere we go. Each day we rush out to our jobs to earn money to make payments on large houses, expensive cars, and maxed-out credit cards, then plan our next shopping trip to continue the cycle. This way of life causes anxiety, depression, and guilt. Though people may not recognize the connection, sleeplessness, fatigue, and irritability can often be traced to worry about how to pay for all the accrued debt related to our stuff. It creates a negative mindset which leads to a negative focus on your days which leads to a negative focus on your life.

You don't have to live this way.
There is a way out.

A Different Way to Live

A few years ago, I stumbled upon an article about minimalism. It's the concept of intentionally living with fewer material possessions. Immediately, I was skeptical. I envisioned odd, eccentric people living with nothing, having no home, and living a boring life. Instead, I learned that minimalism is more about freeing ourselves to do and be what matters in life more than it is about having less stuff.

Owning less is a means to more—
more freedom,
more peace,
more joy,
more time for what matters,
more life.

Minimalism is about recognizing that our stuff distracts us from what is most important.

Minimalism is about understanding that it's not in our possessions we find our greatest joy and source of life.

Minimalism is a path to opening space in our lives to focus on the most important parts of our lives.

What is most important in your life? If you made a list of the most expensive or treasured items you own and a list of what you value most in your life, would your lists have anything in common? Let's not move from this question too quickly. Make those lists, even if only in your head.

I'll wait.

I hope you just had the same "ah-ha" moment I had when I made my lists. I told you in the first chapter of this book that much of what we'd discuss in these pages would be things you already knew but had somehow forgotten along the way. And here we are—again. But this is more than a reminder. This is an invitation to shift the way you think about your stuff and make new choices that will lead you to more of the life you long to live, with less stress, less anxiety, and less debt— while simultaneously giving you more life.

So, what does living more minimally look like?
There are many ways to define minimalism.
Here's my definition:

Choosing to intentionally live with less stuff to create space
for more life.

Just as there are many definitions, there are as many ways to live more minimalistic. There is no set of rules to follow. Some will live out this concept to extremes, owning less than one hundred items. Others, like Jane and me, live a version that fits our lives. We haven't gone to great extremes, but we have shifted the way we think about our possessions and the choices we make about what we own and what we acquire.

That required us to take action.

Why is action necessary?

Isn't the reminder of what's truly important enough?

The morning after my return from Haiti, as I was tying my wing-tip shoes, I too thought the reminder learned in Haiti would be enough to change my thought patterns, my buying habits, how I viewed my excess, and to shift my focus to what really matters in my life.

But over time I forgot... remember?

The Big Purge

After our younger son, Adam, left for college, it was just Jane and me in our home. We immersed ourselves in the concept of minimalism, to test the theory to see if it held any real value that would improve our lives meaningfully. Starting in our basement, we went through every shelf, cabinet, and closet looking for items we thought we could live without. We discovered items we hadn't used in years and found stuff we didn't even remember we owned or where it came from. We found things we didn't even know what they were. We now refer to this project as "the big purge."

We created separate piles of items to give away, sell, or throw away. As we identified items to purge, we built momentum. With momentum came liberation. We grew to enjoy ridding our home of unneeded stuff, becoming almost giddy with each decision to free ourselves of another item. If you've ever cleaned out a closet that was overdue you know that feeling.

Over the next few months, we continued this process throughout every room, closet, cabinet, shelf, and drawer in our house (yes, even our underwear drawers), including the garage. During the months after our purge, something far greater than feeling liberated from stuff set in. We recognized the grip all our stuff had on our lives—a grip previously unnoticed.

Not that we really wanted all this stuff,
we just hadn't realized
that we didn't want it.

We learned that the desire for less is even better than
owning less.

It's difficult to appreciate the burden our stuff creates until we get rid of it. The less stuff we had, the less we wanted more. As our desire to acquire decreased, our desire to pursue what mattered most increased.

Living with fewer possessions clears space in your head to make new choices about living more intentionally into your priorities. Unaware of how much focus we gave to our stuff and the consumption-driven life we were living, when we freed ourselves from that mindset, we cleared headspace and our lives opened to new opportunities to finally make our priorities our priorities (faith, family, and friends).

As we've pursued a life consumed by our priorities, gratitude, the bass note of firm-grip living, has rooted itself deep in our souls and helps us remain focused and positive-minded. Jane and I are the first to admit these new freedoms were the last benefit we ever expected when we first chose to live with fewer material possessions.

Freedom from what enslaves us breathes new life into our
souls.

Real-Life Priorities

When I was told I had an incurable cancer, I had not one thought about my possessions. I didn't think about my home. Not one thought of my car entered my mind. I didn't worry about my closet full of clothes or my high-tech electronics. I had no concern I'd miss my recreational equipment or favorite time-piece should my demise be near. I didn't even think about my sentimental possessions. Instead, my thoughts were on my family, my friends, and God.

- I wanted to watch another sunset on the beach with Jane and hold her hand.
- I wanted to play catch with my sons one more time.
- I wanted to sit on the deck with Jane and friends, sharing a bottle of wine, and talking about our hopes and dreams.
- I wanted to sit in front of a fire with those dear to me and just be present in the moment.
- I wanted to ski the majestic mountains of Utah again, cruising a track with my boys and Jane, fresh powder splashing across my face.
- I wanted to visit Sweden, the land of my ancestors, and learn more about my family heritage.
- I wanted to hug my family and friends and tell them how much I loved them.
- I wanted to discover the deepest, richest parts of knowing my Creator, unearthly connections that had thus far eluded me.
- I wanted to enjoy a meal with friends, the conversation and shared love the only things better than the food.
- I wanted to spend a weekend away with Jane where our thoughts were only us.
- I wanted to tell my sons how proud I was of them.

These and several thousand other similar thoughts were my focus. It's interesting how the arrival of darkness reorients the way we think about what's most important. If you've already had a visit from the darkness, you may have had a similar experience where the 300,000 items in your house suddenly held no value. But regardless of what type of experience you've had, you can shift the way you think about your possessions and make new choices that will radically alter the way you live out your priorities and create a more positive, thriving life right now. As strange as it may sound, living more minimally is one path toward that life—the firm-grip life. But only if you choose to venture down that path will you fully understand how this is possible.

The Journey to Less

So how do you begin living life with less stuff?

First, understand that minimalism is not a one-size-fits-all gig. Despite how much stuff Jane and I parted with, there are minimalists who might view our remaining possessions as far too much. That's okay. This isn't a competition to see who can live with the fewest number of possessions. The goal is to create a shift in the way you think and reduce the number of possessions you own and your desire to acquire, as a pathway to more freedom to pursue what matters most to you. That means you only need to rid yourself of enough to reach that mindset. Now, I suspect like Jane and me, once you discover the unexpected joy of living with less, you won't stop at what you thought was your minimum threshold, but will pursue more freedoms that come as you continue to deepen your investment in minimalism.

So, my advice is simple.
Start.

Don't over-think it. Pick a drawer, a shelf, a small closet, and start. When you purge the first item, congratulate yourself—you've begun your pursuit of living for what matters most in your life! As you continue, you'll find what works and helps you accomplish your goal of living with less to attain a life of more. Jane and I found a couple of ideas helpful to make decisions about our possessions.

First, we ask ourselves two questions:
Does the item serve a useful purpose?
Does the item add value or beauty to our lives?

We've discovered the answers to those questions help us make wise decisions about whether to keep or toss most items.

Second, when deciding about a new purchase, we try to implement what we call the "one in, one out rule." Simply stated, the rule is that for every item we bring into our home that is not replacing a broken or worn-out item, we find an item to remove.

You'll be surprised how these two simple ideas will help you live with fewer possessions.

It's also important to understand you've done nothing wrong. Owning possessions isn't wrong. Wanting or enjoying them isn't wrong. My invitation to you is simply to do something better. We are not our possessions. But somehow, when we don't live with intentionality, our lives don't reflect that truth. Surviving through dark and difficult times is often the reminder that pushes us to make that truth our truth. Whatever has caused you pain, whatever has wounded your soul, whatever dark night of the soul you've endured, those circumstances may just be your catalyst to choose to pursue what matters most and remove those things that distract you from that pursuit.

While that may take many forms, I urge you consider how consumerism and all your stuff may be one of those distractions and how living more minimalistic may be a source of freedom in your life. If you find yourself intrigued by this idea of choosing to live with fewer material possessions and want to dig a bit deeper, I encourage you to explore the work of Joshua Becker, founder of Becoming Minimalist. You can find his insights at www.becomingminimalist.com.

Scripture reminds us that our possessions bring no lasting joy or satisfaction. Jesus said, "Do not lay up for yourselves treasures on Earth, where moth and rust destroy and where thieves break in and steal, but lay up for yourselves treasures in Heaven where neither moth nor rust destroy and where thieves do not break in and steal. For where your treasure is, there will your heart be also." Matthew 6:19-21 (ESV)

I used to think these verses were about moths and rust rotting away our possessions, like holes in our sweaters and rust on our cars, slowly destroying them to the point they have no value. I used to believe the thieves were bad guys who stole from us, like burglars in the night, pick-pockets in the mall, and opportunists who find our cars unlocked. But after my cancer diagnosis, I've seen these words of Jesus with fresh perspectives. These verses aren't about the loss of our items, these verses are about the condition of our hearts. When we're driven by material possessions, and that is the focus of our heart's desire, the moths and rust destroy our hearts, not our stuff. When the thieves break in and steal, they aren't taking our things—they are robbing us of our joy.

It's no surprise this chapter is about the opportunity to make new choices—choices of what we value, where we place our hearts, what we pursue, and how we want to live. This chapter is about shifting the way we think and making new choices about our material possessions that lead us to the firm-grip life. And as we embrace the firm-grip life, it's easier to think differently and make those new choices.

All by deciding to live with less stuff to free our lives to
so… much… more!
Hard to believe?
Then go purge your first item and see for yourself.

14

The Cost of Money

Life Marker: Finances

No one has ever become poor by giving.
—Anne Frank

When I was a young lawyer fresh out of law school, I chose to live and practice law in the small-ish community where I was born and raised. I joined a solo practitioner who had a small but respected law firm, hung my Juris Doctorate diploma and law license on my office wall, and in a moment, I transformed from law student to Attorney at Law. I didn't know much about practicing law even though I'd graduated from law school and passed the bar exam, but I was determined to make my mark.

Being a new lawyer in a small firm didn't come with the option to select the litigation department, real estate department, or corporate department. Our office had one department—it was the "if you have a legal problem and the ability to pay fees, we'll take your case" department. So that's the department I chose. To fill my dance card, I took on a variety of cases from criminal defense to traffic tickets, real estate matters to contract disputes, personal injury cases to worker's compensation claims.

In a small office like ours, family law was a significant part of the caseload. Family law includes divorce cases, child support matters, custody and visitation disputes, and paternity cases. Oddly, *family law* is more about families parting ways than coming together. I always thought we should call it *broken-family law*. Within a few years of beginning my practice, I filled my calendar most days with family law cases. While I didn't enjoy seeing these families part ways, I was determined to help them do so in as healthy a manner as possible to minimize the destructive impact on the lives of parents and children.

During the first twenty years of my practice, approximately fifty percent of my caseload was family law-related. As our office grew from two attorneys to nine, our client base expanded allowing me to shift my practice from family law, but I learned much about people and relationships during those years in family court.

Before becoming a lawyer, had someone had asked me to guess the cause of most divorces and broken relationships, I'd have felt confident that infidelity was the most common cause. Growing apart, inattentiveness, in-law conflict, selfish behaviors, and kid issues would have also been near the top of my guess list. While those and other reasons were the culprits in many cases, the most common demon that ends marriages and relationships is financial problems. The stress of too many bills and not enough money to pay them is a cancer that wove its way into these relationships, resulting in anger, distrust, and a cloud of negativity that overshadowed the marriage to the point of surrender.

When I met with clients facing these financial-driven marriage problems, the distress was written on their faces like a "Danger: High Voltage" sign. They felt helpless and defeated and had given up any hope of a better, more positive future for their relationship. Overwhelmed by financial stress, they waived the white flag.

Who Spends Your Money?

It's difficult to live a positive life narrative
when financial stress weighs you down
with negative thoughts.

If we're honest, most of our financial problems are the product of our prior choices. When pre-qualifying for a home mortgage, the loan officer said, to your delight, you could get a loan for $75,000-$100,000 more than you thought. How did you respond? Maybe you bought a house that cost $100,000 more than you planned. Of course, that came with a monthly payment also larger than planned. But you can afford it, right? The bank employee told you so.

Have you ever gone car shopping for a particular car, only to leave with a fancier, more expensive model, the one with more bells and whistles, sweeter-looking wheels, a much cooler navigation package, and that killer, premium stereo system? The finance guy told you it would only cost a hundred more per month and besides, you work hard—you deserve it!

We do the same thing with our cell phones, televisions, furniture, clothes, and just about everything else we buy; we looked at this compulsive drive for stuff in the last chapter. We spend more than we can afford, trade up too often, and incur more debt than planned.

Sometimes, we even put vacations on our credit cards because we are so stressed and need a break from life, reconciling that we'll just pay for it later, only to discover later, we are under even more stress to pay that credit card balance that includes the vacation that was supposed to ease our stress.

We shop for the sake of shopping like it's some kind of sport or hobby, pull out one of many credit cards and end up with households that have about 300,000 items stuffed and crammed into every space we can find. And when we run out of space, we buy a bigger house with a bigger mortgage payment.

But debt is normal, you might be thinking. Everyone has debt. Who can function without credit cards? Okay, the car was a little more than I planned to spend… okay, a lot more… but I've always wanted a boat. We needed that extra square footage in the house because we'll grow into it. Besides, this is the American dream and that dream costs money!

These thoughts and many others are normal today. But this way of thinking is why many people can't afford more than the minimum monthly payment on their credit card. So, let me ask you—

- Is this what you thought the American dream looked and felt like?
- Did you think you'd lie awake at night wondering how to pay for this dream life?
- Are your finances creating positive or negative energy in your life?

Most American households live paycheck to paycheck regardless of the level of income, proving that it's really not about the amount of money flowing in, but much more about the amount of money flowing out. Remember when you were younger and your paycheck was smaller? You struggled to pay all your monthly bills, but you did, right? As you've grown older, gained more experience, and now earn a larger paycheck, are you still struggling at the end of each month to pay the bills? If so, look around. What changed? And who made those decisions? Here's the truth about our money:

> Most of us make enough money.
> We just don't spend it wisely.
> We've confused what we want with what we need.
> And while we don't like to admit it, how we spend our
> money is a choice only we make.

So, if we control how we spend our money, why do most people live under enormous financial stress? Remember, this book is about living differently, shifting the way we think, and making new choices that will help us create a more positive-focused life—the firm-grip life.

> So, hang on.
> There's hope!

Finding Our Way Out One Choice at a Time

When I graduated from college, I took a job at a bank with a salary of $18,000. I was twenty-two years old and my only possessions fit in a few boxes, the small closet in my one-bedroom apartment and the drawers of the hand-me-down furniture that fit in the back of the smallest U-Haul truck I could rent. I thought I was rich. I couldn't imagine what I'd do with that much money.

My parents said they'd help me create a written budget. At the time I didn't understand why I needed a written budget with all that bank I'd have coming in each month. But they put me through college and the joyful emotions of my recent graduation were still lingering so I thought I'd humor them and go along with their plan.

My mother made columns in a notebook for rent, utilities, food, and gasoline, all normal expenses I expected, appropriate funds allotted to each. Made perfect sense to me. But then she added car insurance that gets paid every six months and created a column for a monthly accrual so the money would be available when the premium was due. Hmmm—I hadn't thought of that. Gifts, renter's insurance, entertainment, dry cleaning, rainy day fund, and other columns I didn't expect were created. My dad added a column for savings and another for charitable giving. My mother adjusted amounts in various columns to make my salary and my expenses match. When we finished, I'm pretty sure my disappointment was only surpassed by my shock over the realization that I was no longer rich.

A few decades have passed since that first budget. I've since earned a doctorate degree, work a professional career with higher earnings and have a wife who has an attractive, corporate compensation package. Yet every January, one of the first tasks in our household is creating a written budget, making appropriate adjustments as needed from last year's budget based on earnings and expected expenses for the new year. I must give credit to Jane who is the master of our budgeting process. She knows how to work our numbers to assure we avoid creating financial stress in our lives. As I've witnessed in my law practice, there's much more at risk than simply overspending.

Over the years, we've worked with other couples to help them learn to create and live within a written budget. Some of these couples were skeptical at first, concerned a written budget would be too constraining, sucking the joy out of their lives. Instead, many told us how grateful they were to discover budgeting isn't about restricting our lives, but about freeing our lives from unnecessary stress and anxiety.

> Your financial life requires choices—purposeful decisions.
> If you don't intentionally choose how you spend your
> money,
> your impulses will choose for you.

When your impulses choose, you buy a larger, more expensive house than needed, the fancier car you never intended to bring home, and the cart full of clothes you really couldn't afford. Whether it be a written budget like ours or a spending plan (net monthly income minus fixed monthly expenses to arrive at how much money remains), planning how you'll spend your money is a critical step to maintaining control of your finances and avoiding the stress of living with unchecked financial decisions.

If you suffer from stress and anxiety created by financial struggles, like every life marker discussed in this book, you can shift the way you think. You can alter the way you view money and make new choices to create a new way to live in a relationship with money. When you choose to do so, you can create a new future without the negativity of financial stress.

Am I telling you to sell your house and downsize? Am I telling you to trade in your car for something less expensive? Am I telling you to get rid of all but one credit card? Not at all. But if that's what you're hearing, maybe there's something larger than my voice at work in your life. Maybe there's an inner voice crying out that it's time to free yourself of the burden of living under financial stress. Certainly, I'm telling you to buy less—as we discussed in the last chapter, we don't even need much of the stuff we already own, so why buy more?

Shifting from long-held patterns of acquisition and accumulation is not an easy shift, but it is possible when we approach the process with new perspectives—firm-grip perspectives.

Firm-Grip Perspectives About Money

For most of us, society and culture shape our perspective about money. We're told to work hard in school so we can get into college so we can get a better job, make more money, and live a better life. This perspective isn't bad. Typically, it's true that working hard in school and in life will create more opportunities. And let's be realistic— opportunity usually comes with more money and more money usually creates more opportunity.

But turn on your radio, television, computer, tablet or phone, and you're bombarded with messages all day about what you need to buy to be happy, fulfilled, accepted, respected, to get ahead, and to live your dream life. Culture teaches us what money can do for us. The sole focus is on how we spend our money: on ourselves. When what money can do for us drives our perspective about money, we live at great risk of becoming a slave to the pursuit of making more and more so we can spend it—on us!

Age and circumstances taught me new perspectives about money. One is to focus on what my money *can't* do for me. The other is to focus on what my money *can* do for others.

Not Enough Zeros

We live in a world that tells us money can resolve most problems. When the hot water heater breaks, we pay a plumber to install a new one. When the transmission on the car acts wonky, we pay a mechanic to repair it. When our kids struggle in school, we hire a tutor to help them learn. When we get strep throat or a broken arm or a rash, we pay the doctor to make it better.

> We've become dependent on money
> as the means of solving our problems—
> until it can't.

When my doctor told me I had a rare and incurable form of the Big C, money was the last thing on my mind. I didn't think about how much I had in my bank account, whether my retirement plan was on track, how I'd pay my sons' next college tuition payments or whether our family budget balanced. Instead, my thoughts were on my family. I didn't want my sons' life stories to include their dad dying while they were still in college. I didn't want Jane to be a widow in the middle of her life.

While we've heard all our lives that money can't buy love and happiness, money also can't cure my cancer or bring back the spouse that walked out on you. No amount of money will ever fix your broken relationships. My friend Julie can't swipe her credit card and bring Jake back, nor can you ever earn enough money to reverse a miscarriage. No matter how many zeros we write on our check, money will never resolve these problems.

I'm not telling you anything here you don't already know. But if we're honest, do our lives really reflect what we say we believe about money? Or do we say that money really doesn't matter, but then live lives that declare money is all that matters? While we say we just want to be happy and live peaceful lives, is all our time spent chasing after the cash so we can just have more?

But...

- What if we lived like we really believed money can't buy the most important things in life?
- What if our daily lives reflected values that truly prioritized faith, family, and friends?
- What if we chose to be grateful for what we now earn rather than living in frustration that we aren't paid more?
- How would our perspectives shift?
- Would we have less stress?
- Would we have more peace?

How I viewed money began to shift after my cancer diagnosis. While I proclaimed money was not the most important thing, the way I lived really didn't reflect my stated beliefs. But when facing the possibility of an earlier than expected death, my perspective on money changed. Possibly, for the first time, I cared about something that money couldn't do for me—I cared about living. I'm talking about waking up on this-side-of-the-dirt-living.

Money, no matter how much of it I could gather, would not keep me alive.

I've not mastered this. In our culture, it takes continual attention, even if you're good at it. I'm still working this out in my firm-grip life. I'm still trying to live in a way that aligns with what I say I believe about money. But I'm determined to do so.

Turning Money into Water

Whether you're holding this book in your hands or reading a digital version, my guess is you had a hot shower today. You also turned on a faucet and washed your hands, brushed your teeth, and enjoyed a cold drink of water. You thought nothing of it when you filled your coffee maker with fresh tap water or flushed your toilet after... well... you know. I have thirteen different sources I can tap for clean water in my home through the turn of a handle or push of a lever or button. I also have 30,000 gallons of it in a pool in my backyard. I never think about access to water until my power goes out, shutting down my well pump.

For most of us, access to clean water has never been a concern. But for almost a billion people in the world, that is not the case.

Several years ago, I was part of a faith community that awakened to the lack of access to clean water for millions living in Africa. We learned of the unimaginable impact that lack of clean water has on Africans. Without access to clean water, villages rely on water sources from local ditches or rivers, water that is polluted and toxic. Consuming polluted water leads to water-borne diseases, devastating human bodies. And without access to medical care, after consuming contaminated water, tens of thousands of African children die from diarrhea each year, a minor medical issue in civilized societies.

Some walk to get clean water carried in small, often contaminated containers. Mothers and their children often walk two to three hours, each way, to get enough clean water for the family's daily needs, subjecting them to violence as they travel. This task prevents the mothers from working to earn much-needed family income and the children from attending school. This daily task of getting water becomes a life focus, one we could not imagine in our civilized culture.

It was unfathomable to us that almost a billion people didn't have a simple, clean glass of water. So, we partnered with an organization called Blood:Water (www.bloodwater.org) and launched a fundraising initiative within our faith community. For one month, we didn't drink any beverage other than water. We saved the money we didn't spend on other beverages and donated that money to build clean water wells in Zambia. People posted photos on social media of tall glasses of water on family dinner tables, shared stories of caffeine withdrawal, and even got their friends and coworkers involved.

A well in Zambia, on average, costs $3000. Our goal was to raise enough funds for two wells. The level of participation in this project grew during the month. The campaign raised far more than we expected. By the end of the month, we had enough money to build seventeen wells! Those seventeen wells now provide clean water to tens of thousands of Africans for decades to come. The lives of thousands of people in Africa, who we'll likely never meet, improved in ways we'll never fully appreciate. Health improved. Family income increased. And kids went back to school to get an education.

When we shift our focus from what our money can do for us
to what our money can do for others,
our new perspectives on money lead us to the firm-grip life.

If you're living with financial stress and don't know how you'll pay this week's bills, this will sound counterintuitive. If you've maxed your credit cards, this will probably go against every basic, financial principle any money expert will tell you. But I'm saying it anyway.

Start giving money to people who need it more than you.

I'm not talking about giving away money to get a benefit on your tax returns. I'm talking about giving money so that other people's lives can shift from despair to hope, from ruin to restoration, and even from death to life. It doesn't have to be large sums.

You just need to give for one purpose—
to help another human being.

None of us individually gave enormous sums to build wells in Zambia. But together, we saved lives and restored families. We gave them hope for a better life and a real future. There is significance in that. There is something right and good and human about refusing to let another human suffer when we can help. There is something that stirs in the soul when we love and help our brothers and sisters when they can't help themselves. It changes us, shapes us, forms us into what we were created to be—an extension of the Divine here on Earth... as it is in Heaven.

You may not have much to give. That's okay. Give one dollar. Find a way to help someone who needs it more than you and give one dollar. It's not the amount of money you give that will change your perspective on money but the impact your giving has on another person's life. When you truly begin to recognize what your money can do for others, your money feels different in your pocket, the numbers in your checkbook take on new meaning.

When your money no longer only represents what you can gain, but what you can give, you've discovered a path to a positive future for you and our world. It may take a long time to alter the course of your finances. So why not start right now? With a decision to act today. Just one step at a time. With each step, you are living the firm-grip life—positive and hopeful.

15

Judge of the World

Life Marker: Judging Others

*Never judge another knight without first knowing the
strength and cunning of the dragons he fights.*
—Richelle E. Goodrich, *Slaying Dragons*

I'm part of the O.J. Simpson generation. I was a young adult
during what is often called the trial of the twentieth century. For those
of you also of this generation, please indulge me a moment to get the
youngsters in the room caught up.

O.J. Simpson was a professional football player in the 1970s.
He rose to super-star status and was inducted into the Pro Football
Hall of Fame in 1985. After retiring his cleats, he had a successful
career in acting and broadcasting. He had a charming smile and warm
personality. His life appeared perfect.

Until he was arrested and charged with murder.

In 1994, the state of California charged O.J. Simpson with killing
his former wife and her friend in a brutal slaying. Ninety-five million
people watched as television stations interrupted the 1994 NBA

Playoffs to broadcast the low-speed chase that ended in his capture and arrest.

The trial lasted nine months. Opening arguments to the jury lasted four days. The prosecution called seventy-two witnesses over ninety-nine days of testimony. O.J.'s defense team called fifty-four witnesses who testified over thirty-four days of trial. The prosecution offered 488 exhibits into evidence while the defense presented 369 exhibits. The state of California used nine prosecutors while O.J.'s defense team comprised eleven attorneys. After four days of closing arguments, the jury deliberated only four hours to reach its verdict. Four hours. From a lawyer's perspective, if a jury only requires four hours to reach a unanimous verdict after listening to 126 witnesses testify over 133 days, it's safe to say the jury was confident in its verdict.

Although the trial was televised, come on, who can sit and watch a nine-month trial on TV? I couldn't. I had a life to live, a job to do, a wife to spend time with, kids to raise, grass to mow, and only about a gazillion other things to do. So, like the rest of the nation, most of what I saw was video snippets on the news, handpicked by the broadcasting network, usually the most salacious parts of the testimony.

Everyone was captivated by this trial. And of course, everyone formed an opinion regarding O.J.'s guilt or innocence, and most were more than willing to share their opinion whenever the trial came up in conversation. Most of the people I spoke with were confident of O.J.'s guilt. But that didn't surprise me. It was obvious the media broadcast those portions of the trial that pointed most toward guilt. A guilty O.J. made for a much better news story than an innocent O.J.

Since I was an attorney at the time, many people wanted to know my opinion about O.J.'s guilt or innocence. I always answered the same way— "I've not been in the courtroom. I haven't heard the witnesses. And I haven't seen the trial exhibits. So, I can't offer a fair opinion on whether the evidence proves guilt beyond a reasonable doubt. And neither should you offer such an opinion unless you've heard and seen all the evidence." The typical response was a puzzled look of disappointment that I didn't agree with their opinion of guilt. Hey, what were they expecting? They asked a lawyer!

When the jury returned its not guilty verdict, many were shocked and angry. He was guilty. Everyone knew he was guilty. Just ask them—they'll tell you so. Based on their limited knowledge, they were confident.

They decided.
They cast their judgment.
We always judge, don't we?

Judging others seems to be America's pastime, like a sport or hobby. Maybe it's always been this way, but my perception is that in recent years people have become hypercritical of each other. I suspect increased access to information through technology, including the internet and social media, contributes to this heightened trend of sizing everyone up. Information, regardless of its veracity, is available to us twenty-four hours a day. We have more information flooding into our daily lives than at any other time in human history. The problem is that far too many of us believe too much of what we hear or read while failing to consider we may not have all the information needed to truly understand the issue or person.

We've all been guilty of casting premature judgment.

Let's bring it closer to home.

When we see a news story about a local crime, we usually get little information: the name of the accused, a mugshot depicting the individual at less than their best, and the crime allegedly committed. If we're lucky, we get a few allegations, but rarely enough to prove guilt. Yet, if we're honest, most of us presume the accused is guilty, don't we? Why else would law enforcement have arrested the person? Why else would the story be in the news? Why else would a judge and lawyers and the court system spend all that time on it? If pressed, we might admit we'd need more information to prove the guilt of the accused. We'd all likely agree the accused is entitled to a day in court. And we'd all agree that under our constitution, a person is innocent until proven guilty. That's what we're taught, right?

That's not how it worked for O.J.
And it's not how it usually works today, is it?

But I Didn't Do It

Jane and I had just arrived home from work when there was a knock on our door. I was a young lawyer at the time so I was changing out of my business suit. I looked out the window to see a police car in our driveway while I was pulling on a pair of jeans. As I opened the door, I expected to see our friend, a local police officer who stopped by for frequent visits. Instead, there stood a police officer I didn't know, my attention quickly drawn to his hand firmly gripping his gun.

Have you ever had an experience

when within the first milliseconds
you knew it would not be a good experience?
This was one of mine.

The officer said my full name, asking me to confirm my identity. Then he asked if I owned a green sport utility vehicle, which I did. Next, he asked if I was just at a particular gas station, which I was. My concern growing, he told me a man matching my physical description, driving a vehicle like mine, bearing my license plate number, was just reported for pulling a silver handgun on two young girls at the gas station I just left.

He asked me to step outside and keep my hands in plain view, still gripping his firearm.

Heart racing, I knew I was not in a good situation. I'd been practicing law long enough to know that prosecutors charge many crimes based only upon the statements of alleged victims. I understood that reality as most criminals don't commit their crimes in view of many witnesses. I also knew if he arrested me, the crime charged would be a felony. And I knew that as an attorney in a small community, if they charged me, no matter the outcome of the case, my legal career was likely finished. But there was one other thing I knew...

I didn't do it.

Soon it was clear there was another police officer involved. He was with my two young accusers and their parents, radio calls going back and forth between him and the officer standing in front of me, trying to sort out the details. From the sound of their early conversation, and confirmation from the officer standing in front of me saying he *"had the guy,"* an unplanned visit to our local jail seemed to be in my evening schedule with a free ride in a police car.

Desperate to turn the tide of this wave before it crashed down on me and my legal career, I told the officer I was a local attorney, had not committed this crime, and if he arrested me, my career would be over. I told him where I worked, that I was born and raised in this community, and had no criminal record. That information slowed him down and bought me time to try to save my future.

Over the course of the next couple hours, I plead my case, allowed the officer to search my car and home and even showed him the only handgun I owned, black in color, tucked away in a nightstand, dusty and obviously untouched for years. Slowly, I built momentum in my favor, as the officer expressed casual doubt in the report from the accusers. But no matter how hard I worked to convince him, there was nothing I could do to get this officer into my head, the only place where the certainty of my innocence existed.

Eventually, after inconsistencies arose in their story, my young accusers admitted they fabricated the story because they were late getting home and didn't want to be in trouble with their parents. So, they picked me as the victim of their scheme, just a poor sap filling his fuel tank at the end of a workday.

I didn't go to jail that night. I didn't get charged with a crime. My name and mugshot didn't appear in the local news. And I didn't lose my career. Before the officer left, I asked if, prior to the girls' confession, he thought I did it. He said he wasn't sure but had been leaning toward arresting me.

It's chilling how much was riding on one man's judgment of me.

Better Than You

Human propensity to judge others exists not only in matters of the law like O.J.'s case or my near brush with the criminal justice system. There is no area of life that isn't subject to our predisposition to judge. We judge others based on their politics, opinions, race, and ethnicity, level of education, sexual orientation, homes, income, religious affiliation, physical appearance, parenting skills, social status, and just about any other issue we choose. But our proclivity to judge doesn't stop with life's largest issues. We're just as likely to judge others over matters of little consequence. Here are some examples:

- A friend buys a new car and we think, *he can't afford that car!*
- Your neighbor joins a gym and your thought is, *she didn't stick with it last year—doubtful she will this year.*
- A friend posts a vacation photo on social media and all you can think is, *quit trying to make your life appear so awesome.*
- A driver cuts you off and you scream, "IDIOT!"

I've struggled with this life marker. I've judged with the best of them. And I've come to this conclusion: Being the judge of the world is exhausting. The need to always be right, to prove others wrong, to feel superior or believe others are inferior is heavy, drains our souls, and leaves us empty and unfulfilled. And that's where judging is birthed, isn't it—in our need to feel better about ourselves? When we scream MORON! at another driver who ticked us off because he left his turn signal on too long, we're saying—-*I'd never do such a stupid thing.... idiot! You're a bad driver and I'm not; therefore, I'm better than you.*

I know.

It seems insignificant and silly, doesn't it?

But little actions of judgment like this, repeated many times a day, over extended periods of time (like a lifetime, for example), work their way into our lives and create a negative atmosphere in our soul, leading to negative thoughts. How did you feel after you screamed at the other driver? Full of positive mojo and good vibes? Are you overflowing with positivity when you mentally slam your awkward co-worker who tells stupid jokes trying to fit in at the office? Does that inside-your-head sneer toward your friend who bragged a bit too much about her kid help you live a more positive-focused life? Of course not!

It's difficult to live the firm-grip life when we stand in constant judgment of others.

There's one thing certain—we're all guilty of casting judgment. Judging others is the evil twin sister of comparing ourselves to others. Left unchecked, we'll judge others with such frequency that we become numb to the fact we are even doing it. Without intentional effort to curb our tendency to judge, we'll do so multiple times a day to multiple people we encounter. Like a cancer that grows and strengthens its grip, over time, judging others fosters a negative impact, deeply rooted in our souls, that ever so slowly drains our joy and seeds bitterness, anger, and even hatred. There are few people who wake up in the morning and decide today is the day they will become negative and hateful. Like cancer, these evils take far more time to grow and invade our lives. Judging others is a fertilizer that fosters that growth.

The Drive

It was the day before my surgery. Jane and I were headed to Indianapolis for my final pre-operative appointment with my surgeon. I was behind the wheel, my head thick with too many thoughts, none of which were the road in front of me or the driver behind me. I'm not sure if I was thinking about the fact that in less than twenty-four hours the surgeon would cut my neck open from ear to ear and tack the skin back over my face to have access to my inner neck. It's possible I was focused on my sons, wondering if they were in danger of this disease. Maybe I was worried about being under anesthesia for eight hours. I could have been wondering if I would be alive much longer or whether my end, if near, would be painful. I may have been thinking about how quickly my life had changed.

Whatever I was thinking about it wasn't my sub-limit speed or the driver behind me who apparently had been wanting to get around me for a while. Once he had the chance, he whipped by, engine roaring, front end heaving from the extra horsepower propelling him past me. As he made his way around, he gestured with his arm as if to say, *Come on buddy, get going. I haven't got all day!* My immediate thought was, *Dude! You have no clue what I'm going through!*

As soon as that thought left the brain cells that formed it, a new thought arrived, this one bringing a shameful revelation: *How many times have I cast similar judgment on someone, clueless to what they might be going through?*

Living the firm-grip life means working to stop constantly judging other people. We have to walk away from our *us versus them* mindset. We have to stop figuring out who's in and who's out of whatever preconceived club we've invented in our minds. We have to quit filtering our view of others through our ideas, beliefs, and opinions and value people for theirs, even when they differ from ours.

One-Step Plan

While I'm certain there are professional and clinical methods to get deep into our psyche at what drives us to judge others, maybe even some mood-altering medications to help fix some emotional baggage, I will leave that to others with different letters behind their name than mine. Instead, I want to offer a practical, easy-to-follow, easy-to-remember, one-step method to help us become less judgmental.

Grace.
Simply offer grace.

Every time you realize you're judging someone who walks in the room, says something you don't agree with, takes an opposing political position, or lives a lifestyle different from yours, offer grace. When someone brags about their life, or kid, or career, or money, offer grace. When someone posts on social media about the amazing time they're having, on an exotic vacation they're on, or whatever else makes you jealous, offer grace. When you're tempted to condemn an accused in a matter you know little about, spew venomous words about a politician you don't like, or belittle a group of people protesting something you don't understand or agree with, offer grace.

Grace, grace, grace.
Offer it in abundance, over and over again.

Just as it's hard to live a negative-focused life when our hearts are full of gratitude, it's equally difficult to be judgmental when our gesture toward others is grace.

But they don't deserve grace, you say.
But they really are wrong, you protest.
I know.
Offer grace anyway.

Listen, I'm not suggesting that offering grace means we must agree with the other person, their actions or decisions, but we can disagree with the issue, yet still offer grace to the person. There's a big difference, a difference we humans have lost somewhere along our way. When we offer grace to the person, despite our disagreement with the issue, we're acknowledging...

- that we don't know what dragons they're trying to slay in their lives.
- that we don't know the pain from which their actions, views or opinions come.
- that they are worthy of second chances.
- that we don't know if they're on their way to surgery for a rare, incurable cancer.

Offer grace.

"But grace was given to each one of us according to the
measure of Christ's gift." Ephesians 4:7 (ESV)

The only reason we can offer grace to others is that grace was first offered to us by the One who created us. The Divine suspends judgment when we say hurtful things, act selfishly, and are unkind to others. Instead, he offers grace. When we brag about ourselves, take up a cause not everyone agrees with or we were wrong about, or stay in the left lane wanting to get in front of as many people as possible before we have to merge right, he offers grace. When we get in an online argument with people over political opinions (a lesson I've learned), he offers grace. When our faith communities are more interested in determining who's in and who's out of the Kingdom of God than sharing the love of God, he offers grace, grace that never runs empty.

Grace—not judgment.

Grace is an amazing thing in the hands of a loving God.
It's equally amazing in human hands
when we offer it to others—
freely, unmerited, and especially when undeserved.

Offering grace requires that we shift how we relate to and interact with other people. We must stop perceiving everyone as our competition—stop regarding the person we disagree with as wrong— stop treating people who offend us as our enemy. We must learn to see everyone as someone who's fighting demons we know nothing of, possibly carrying deep wounds from the battle. We have to view the driver who cut in front of us as a person who may be on his way to the hospital to say goodbye to a dying father—because he might be.

It's often said we find what we're looking for. We can look for the bad in people, and find it, or we can choose to look for the good in people, which is always there to be discovered. Grace creates space to find the good in people.

But grace, like judgment, is a choice.

We can choose to judge
or we can choose to offer grace.

I need frequent reminders of the grace God has called me to extend to every person I meet. Since the temptation to judge others is a battle I fight every day, I'm grateful to have daily reminders to offer grace in place of judgment. And usually, my reminder comes from remembering the darkness I've experienced in my life, a reminder that everyone has their own kind of darkness, and that they deserve grace. How unexpected that surviving our own darkness can be a catalyst to show grace to others.

Want to increase your ability to offer grace to others? Then choose to live the firm-grip life. The firm-grip lifestyle helps us put others before ourselves. When we do that, we can more easily shift from judgment and choose grace—again and again and again.

16

The Sacred Tribe

Life Marker: Relationships

It is the friends you can call at 4 a.m. that matter.
—Marlene Dietrich

On the day after my diagnosis, Jane and I were to attend a post-holiday party. It was a formal event—black tie optional, long elegant gowns—hosted by our local hospital, where my wife was a member of the hospital foundation's board of directors. Many physicians would be in attendance, some to receive awards for their efforts in medicine during the past year.

Our immediate thought was to skip the event, our minds too detached for an evening of pageantry and celebration. I couldn't imagine engaging in small-talk conversations with others about the weather, current events or how nice everyone looked in their formal attire when our minds were still stunned from the news of my diagnosis, wondering how advanced it was, thinking about next steps and whether I was on limited time. My experience is that those type of discussions over cocktails and hors d'oeuvres tend to unsettle people, quickly excusing themselves, scurrying off in favor of less stressful dialogue. After much debate, we went thinking maybe a night out would help distract us.

I remember walking in the room, familiar faces everywhere. My first thought: *None of them know.* The air felt thick, shallow inhales followed by labored exhales. *How was I ever going to get through this? How do I engage, show interest as I hear about someone's kid hitting the winning shot earlier that day in a basketball game? How do I even find the strength to stand on my feet and look someone in the eye as they tell me about their new job?* My next thought: *I'm in a room full of doctors who heal people for a living and probably none of them can heal me.*

I survived the evening, fake smile on my face and finding just enough breath to exhale some academy award-worthy laughter when someone told a joke. I experienced many emotions that evening, but none more real, transcendent, or overwhelming as that feeling of being alone—utterly alone. In a crowd of hundreds of people, some I'd known for decades, I felt alone as if invisible to all in the room but Jane. Only she saw me, felt my grief, shared my fear, knew my uncertainty. But even then, there was a solitary place Jane couldn't enter with me—a place that only permitted admission for one.

A cancer diagnosis creates a lonely space no one else can enter, its margins too thin for more than one. But I suspect many paths of darkness are like that, including yours. We're forced into isolation by our pain and suffering—a place we must forge, finding our way, finding our strength, finding our next breath, on our own, guided only by the urgings of the Divine. It's a terrifying space, yet one filled with simultaneous beauty, a paradox I can't explain. But wherever I've encountered the Divine in my life, even in my darkest places, there's been a light, sometimes barely bright enough to light my path, but always enough to see my next step.

Despite this lonely space I had to navigate, the Divine my only companion, my pilgrimage with cancer lead me to new understandings about the gift of relationships. I gained new perspectives about meaningful people in my life who, although they couldn't enter my solitary, thin space, served as north stars who kept me leaning toward hope. God put people in my life, long before my cancer diagnosis, who spoke love, hope and truth into my life.

I'm talking about people who transcend a common notion of friendship. I'm talking about connections so sacred you feel them in your soul—people whose voice in your life brings such wisdom and love that your heart vibrates long after they've left—people you feel present, even when they're not.

I'm talking about people who are your tribe.

The firm-grip life is about finding your tribe.

Created to Connect

God created us to live in community, to have meaningful relationships and connections with other humans who bear the image of our Creator. Yet, modern society has confused the concept of community and friendship. According to my social media apps, I have 1,460 friends. Some of these cyber friends I've never met, connecting through common interests, others with whom I share the bond of my particular type of cancer, and still others whose origins of friendship

I'm uncertain. There's nothing wrong with these modern means of connection as long as we understand them for what they are.

They're not our tribe.

A cancer diagnosis not only rocks the world of the one hosting the cancerous evil but the lives of those close to them. Family and friends go through their own form of diagnosis and have to process the news as if they themselves have an illness. Just like cancer patients, some handle it better than others. I had a core group of friends, those in my inner circle, come alongside Jane and me. These friends were present with us, day and night, in-person and through various communications, always assuring us we were not in this alone.

When I felt overwhelmed, a timely call or encouraging text would arrive, keeping me off the edge. Frequent visits and evenings together were constant reminders of their love and support. Sometimes they offered no words, only their presence as if our souls had their own conversation, silent to our ears, yet life-giving to the journey I traveled. And while I treasured their presence, each seemed to know there was that thin space I had to live alone, a place they couldn't enter, that place where I had to do my interior work by myself. But they knew they offered something that helped me navigate that space. Your tribe always knows what you need.

It's said that dark times reveal true friends. While many people offer their thoughts and prayers, the friends who offer you their soul, the ones who sit and cry with you, who's heart shatters with yours, are rare and few.

Those kinds of people showed up in my life.
Those people are my tribe.

Sweatpants and T-Shirts

Every relationship creates energy, either negative or positive. There's no such thing as a neutral relationship. And each person brings a negative or positive energy to the relationship. Every interaction you have with another human being will leave you feeling energized and positive or depleted and negative—sometimes a little, sometimes a lot. Think about the people you spend time with at work, in social settings, at faith gatherings, or even in your own home. You may not have considered this, but think about how you feel after spending time with those people. Do you walk away inspired, encouraged and hopeful, or dejected, discouraged, and hopeless? How do you think they feel after spending time with you?

We all have negative people in our lives. We can't escape that reality as we have many relationships required by our circumstances— work or family relationships, for example. Sometimes we're around purely toxic people, those who bring nothing but conflict and chaos, those who offer only negative energy and discord. Relational conflict is unavoidable and part of the human experience. If relational turmoil doesn't impact our lives in some manner, we're probably not living much of a relational life and are spending too much time alone.

It's important to remember, though, that we can still learn from toxic and negative people. Every engagement with another human offers opportunity to learn, grow, and improve. But if we're too busy judging them, we miss those opportunities. We can and should offer respect and love to negative and toxic people, even if we need to do so from afar, behind boundaries established to protect ourselves from their negative influence. Despite our unavoidable interactions with negative and toxic people, they're simply not our tribe; so, we need not concern ourselves with the angst these relationships would otherwise create. Firm-grip attitudes help us create healthy perspectives on difficult relationships by pointing our focus back to the life-giving relationships of our tribe.

We all also have casual friendships. These are the people we know, run into occasionally at the coffee shop or grocery store. They're likable people. Some are people we grew up with and have known most of our lives. Others are pleasant people at work, folks we serve on a local board with, or who live in our neighborhood. We offer them our support in their difficult times and they may offer prayers for us in ours. They're good people and we care about them, wish them well, and desire good things for them. But the relationship remains casual and without a deep, meaningful connection. They're friends... but they're not our tribe.

Relationships with people in your tribe are different. These are next-level relationships. In the tribe, there is a deep, meaningful connection that you can often feel far more than you can explain. But you just *know*. There is a comfort with people in your tribe that doesn't exist in your other relationships, a comfort that feels like coming home at the end of a long day and changing into sweatpants and an old t-shirt.

Drain Tubes

"For better or worse" is tribe language. There is no tribal bond thicker than marriage. In a world that has forsaken marriage as a rusty, worn-out institution of inconvenience and misrepresents love, Jane reminded me of the raw, unconditional love that is foundational not only to a marriage but to the deep level of connection found only in the tribe. While processing her response to my diagnosis, Jane, often through action more than words, loved me in ways I'd never imagined possible when I said, *"I do,"* many years ago. Of all the ways Jane loved me during the darkest days of this journey, there was one thing she did that, in the strangest way, has been the most beautiful expression of love she's ever offered me.

I'm easily grossed out. I have a weak stomach and extremely sensitive gag reflex. I often gag while brushing my teeth. I'm talking loud, shoulder shrugging, tears-rolling-down-my-cheeks gags. Jane laughs at me... while I'm gagging. After my surgery, I discovered something far more disgusting than a toothbrush too far back on my tongue—drain tubes!

When I woke from surgery, three rubber tubes protruded from my neck like cords from an entertainment system. In the hospital, they were attached to vacuum pumps on the wall. Without getting too gross, drain tubes allow fluids that form after surgery to drain, reducing swelling, and lowering the risk of infection and complications. A clear-ish, red-ish, gross-ish fluid. As much as I love my surgeon, drain tubes were a detail he forgot to tell me about before surgery.

Before I left the hospital, the docs removed one of the drain tubes. They disconnected the other two from the wall vacuum and attached them to small, flexible suction bulbs, that clipped to my shirt and hung on my chest. I wondered why they clipped the bulbs to my shirt, but soon discovered the answer. Without clips, the suction bulbs, now carrying the weight of the drained fluids, pull on the skin at the site of insertion, causing significant discomfort. I looked like a science project gone bad.

The doctor *kindly* allowed me to keep these drain tubes for an entire week. As the bulbs filled with fluid, they had to be emptied.

Too gross a task to ask Jane to perform, I was relieved when she volunteered to do so. I couldn't even watch, sitting still, eyes closed, going to the happy place in my mind to avoid a full-tilt gag session.

Showering was a different challenge. Since the clips didn't attach to bare skin, the bulbs just hung, pulling at the skin. Once again, Jane came to my rescue. Our shower has a small corner seat. I sat there, holding the bulbs in my hands, eyes closed because I couldn't risk getting a glimpse of the suction bulbs full of my neck fluids for fear of throwing my body into gag-induced convulsions. While I sat there pathetic, helpless and useless, Jane used the shower sprayer to hose me down and clean me up. I called these my doggie baths.

I can laugh at it now, but her love and compassion deepened our connection in ways no romantic dinner over candles ever could.

That act of helping me shower reshaped my understanding of deep connection, taught me new levels of love, and helped me comprehend the difference between ordinary relationships and relationships that exist within the tribe.

Jane is part of my tribe.

The rest of my tribe has included a variety of family members, lifelong friends, and some who have been part of my life for a season. Tribe members may come and go—that's okay. I've learned to embrace each for the gift they are for as long as God has placed us together.

My tribe also comprises people who are mentors in my life, others who serve as spiritual guides who have helped Jane and me in our faith journeys and in our marriage, always pointing us to what is true, and still others who simply "get us." There are other couples that are common tribe-sters to both Jane and me. And within my tribe are a handful of men who are my brothers if not in blood, in spirit. We love each other without condition. We have a connection that transcends the words that would describe the depth of our bond. Many of these relationships are forged by a common faith in God. I call them my Five-Finger-Friends because I can count them on one hand. I've learned that if I can count to five the number of friends that love me that well, then I'm truly blessed.

Regardless of who my tribe members are, there is always one thing in common between us. We love each other deeply, regardless of what happens in our lives and no matter what comes our way.

Finding Your Tribe

Tribe-level friends can come from many places; family, social groups, faith communities, work places and any other relational setting. It's not about where you connect, it's about how you connect. While no one individual will likely display every attribute below, are there people in your life who display any of the following?

- They live an inspired life that inspires yours.
- They live highly motivated and motivate you.
- They are grateful.
- They don't waste time complaining.
- They live purposefully and intentionally.
- They avoid drama and negativity.
- They encourage you to pursue your passions.
- They always remind you of what is true and good and right.
- They always cheer for you.
- They bring positive energy.
- They bring out the best in you—always.
- They love you unconditionally.

- They empower you.
- They support and believe in you.
- They always show up in your life.
- They get you.
- They reflect the presence of the Divine.

Look around your life.

Who are the people that come to mind as you read that list?

Who are the people that seem to show up every time you need them, no matter what? Who are those that lift your soul, boost your confidence, encourage and inspire you, and always love you even when you're not acting loveable? Who are your north stars that help you find your way through that dark, solitary, thin space? Who are the people that seem to be living the firm-grip life, even though they don't call it that? Those people? They're your tribe. If there's only one person, start there. That's your tribe. If you find your life void of these people, maybe it's time to expand your relationship circle to seek and include those who would nourish your soul.

When you find your tribe, you always *know* because you feel different—inspired, safe, connected, and known. They are the people who speak truth into your life and whose truth you welcome, who encourage you to be authentically you and will be authentic around you. They breathe life into you that lingers long after your time together ends. Their presence calms you and informs your soul that everything will be okay—or at least if not okay, you won't be alone. Finding your tribe is like sitting in your favorite chair—you know you're home. This is what the tribe does for each other because tribe-level relationships are sacred. And that sacredness is something you feel and just *know* is real.

Living through this cancer journey created new perspectives into the unique, yet significant difference between friendships and the bonds of the tribe. I grew a newfound, deepened love for my tribe, a soul-stirring that created connections Divinely appointed. I long to be with my tribe because I understand I need them and they need me. We belong to each other. We're woven together to be stronger than any of us on our own.

You need your tribe too.
And they need you, far more desperately than you may realize.

You probably have a lot of relationships with people that bring positive energy into your life. But if you want to create and live the firm-grip life, find your tribe. And when you do, love them hard. Never take them for granted. Be intentional about spending time together. Tell them what they mean to you. Show up for them. Be the person who drops everything when they need you. And thank God for them every day because they are a treasure poured into your life.

But just don't expect everyone in your tribe to give you a doggie bath!

17

To Speak of it No More

Life Marker: Forgiveness

One forgives to the degree that one loves.
—Francois de La Rochefoucauld

I'm a fiercely loyal person.

Jane says I'm sometimes loyal to a fault. That may be true, but it's how I'm wired. When I develop a friendship, I often go all in and have that person's back, even to my personal expense or pain. There have been occasions when my loyalty was, admittedly, misplaced.

I've noticed one problem with living fiercely loyal is that sometimes I struggle to forgive. I have an unrealistic expectation of loyalty from others. But I want to live within the dual current of forgiveness, where I can receive and grant forgiveness freely, making relationships a priority above all else.

As I strive to make the daily choice to live the firm-grip life, I've learned that withholding forgiveness is a huge obstacle. It became clear that living the firm-grip life, knowing I'm held firmly by the Divine, requires that I live with a loose grip on my grudges toward others—that forgiveness is the better path. After my cancer diagnosis, a shift occurred in my thinking that helped me recognize the negative, weighty burden we carry when we refuse to forgive others.

Several years ago, a person did something that upset me. This wrong wasn't committed against me, but against a friend. My friend suffered a deep wound, but I also hurt badly, as if I'd been the target of the wrong. It pained me to see my friend hurting. So, I hurt for and with this friend. I carried the grudge for my friend and soon harbored anger and resentment against the wrongdoer. As I watched my friend heal and forgive, I couldn't. I didn't. I withheld forgiveness for several years. I carried that with me every day.

Then... cancer showed up.
Cancer, once again, began to change me.

Shortly after my diagnosis, I awoke one morning feeling burdened, a crushing weight, physically palpable in my chest. It arrived with a haunting angst that gripped me. Immediately, I knew it wasn't physical—it had nothing to do with the cancer— yet it had everything to do with the cancer. The path ahead was obvious. That path pointed to one person—this person from whom I'd withheld forgiveness. It was time. Withholding my forgiveness was a cancer in my soul, slowly destroying me, creating a negative shadow over my life, even though I hadn't been aware of the shadow's presence.

I told Jane I was wrong all these years to withhold my forgiveness from this person. I had to set them free. The uncertainty of my future caused by cancer now turned to an urgency to release this person from the wrongs of the past—wrongs I allowed to scar my soul and wound my spirit. The burden was heavy; I couldn't take the chance I'd run out of time to forgive.

That morning I reached out and forgave the person. I also sought forgiveness for wrongfully withholding it in the first place. Graciously, the person forgave me—instantly. And right there, it was done.

We agreed to speak of it no more.

It was over.

We were both free.

Living the firm-grip life gives us courage to forgive.

Currents and Confusion

"…and forgive us our debts, as we also have forgiven our debtors…" Matthew 6: 12 (NIV)

There's a current to forgiveness, a flow in and out. Like an electrical current flows into our homes, then out into our devices, forgiveness flows into our lives from the Divine and others who grant forgiveness to us but is intended to flow out of us to others. We want forgiveness. We crave that inward current because we know we mess up—we hurt others—we cause pain. We experience relief and gratitude when someone forgives our offense. Yet, having freely received forgiveness, many of us struggle to offer the outflowing current to others.

Forgiveness is easily misunderstood, creating confusion that contributes to our inability to offer forgiveness to others. This leads to this question—

Where did we get the idea that forgiving someone means everything is now fine?

I think our confusion began when we were young and a parent or teacher told another child to say "I'm sorry" for saying something mean or kicking us in the shin. Afterward, we were told to respond with "I forgive you." Then the teacher forced us to hug it out, making everything okay and back to normal. The problem is when we get older, it's not always easy, or right, to hug it out and go back to normal after deep hurts pierce and wound our soul. Often, we aren't ready to go back to normal, certain that normal may never return to the relationship. So, we withhold the outward current of forgiveness.

To help our understanding of forgiveness, let's start with what forgiveness is not.

1. Forgiveness is not dependent on the offender's apology, an expression of remorse, or even acknowledgment of wrongful conduct. Those are actions only another person can take. News flash—you can't ever control the actions of another person. If you always wait for an apology before offering forgiveness, there'll be times you'll carry your burden the rest of your life—because some people will never apologize. Apologies are not our responsibility. But nothing and no one can stop us from taking action to offer forgiveness. We control our actions. Forgiveness is solely our responsibility.

2. Forgiveness is not approval of the wrongful conduct. It wasn't okay that we got kicked in the shin on the playground, yet when the teacher made us hug it out, we felt like we condoned it, making it okay to be the victim again during the next recess. Regardless of your decision to forgive, the conduct was wrong and will always be wrong. Forgiveness doesn't grant approval, forgiveness actually proclaims the

conduct as wrong, yet releases both parties from the soul-weight of what occurred.

3. Forgiveness does not eliminate the consequences of the wrong. When a grieving mother forgives the person who murdered her child, the murderer still goes to prison. You can forgive someone for all sorts of atrocities, yet justice may still require imposition of consequences.

4. Forgiveness is not always reconciliation. Forgiving a spouse for infidelity doesn't mean the relationship can continue if trust can't be restored. After forgiving a business partner for embezzlement, it may be impossible to continue in business together. Some relationships are simply too toxic to expose yourself to the risk of further pain and sorrow. But you can still choose to forgive.

5. Despite what you may have been told all your life, forgiveness is not always forgetting. In some relationships, you may forgive and forget, moving forward as if nothing occurred—like my friend who quickly forgave me for withholding my forgiveness, we chose to speak of it no more. But that's not always possible. Sometimes you *need* to remember so you can establish healthy boundaries going forward to protect yourself. Some people are toxic, yet you have no choice but to remain in a relationship with them. They may be a parent, sibling, co-worker, in-law, or even child. It's simply not possible to end the relationship. So, remembering the wrong, even though forgiven, may be necessary, not to continue to hold the offense, but to establish healthy boundaries to prevent future harm.

The Journey of Forgiveness

Here's what I think forgiveness is.

1. Forgiveness is a process. A few years ago, there were two people I needed to forgive, both involved in the same offense. After a considerable time, I finally extended forgiveness, but as a dog returns to its vomit, I kept coming back to negative thoughts about them, creating the need to forgive them over and over, day after day. This went on for months. But over time, I slowly thought less about the offense, until finally, my forgiveness achieved a completeness. Fully loaded forgiveness sometimes takes a while, maybe years, even decades. That's okay. The key is that you continue through the process. Along the way, celebrate each step as a victory. If you wish them less harm today than you did yesterday, that's progress. That's the reality of the process of forgiveness.

2. Forgiveness is grace extended even when not deserved. Extending forgiveness is only possible because of the grace we've already received from God and others. "But they don't deserve my forgiveness," you protest. But you do? Do you deserve the grace of forgiveness from the Divine, from those you've wronged? Forgiveness is nothing if not grace. Forgiveness doesn't exist without grace. Extending forgiveness to others is the best of what it means to be human as we pass to others the grace, mercy, and love extended to us, even when we didn't deserve it. "Forgive them Father for they know not what they do." Sound familiar?

3. Forgiveness is a declaration that the cycle of revenge and getting even ends here. When we withhold forgiveness, it's often because we're more interested in seeking revenge. Revenge is a myth—like redemptive violence—that somehow, we can redeem a wrong with another wrong.

> How will we ever know if we got even?
> Is it a feeling?
> Will the other side admit defeat?
> Unlikely.

It will only escalate the situation and create more conflict, whether active or passive. Either way, you're not free. Pursuing revenge only invites the cycle of revenge and conflict to continue. When we choose to forgive, it ends this cycle, creating peace. Sure, you may bear some level of pain to end the cycle, but you become a peacemaker and end the conflict, creating space to heal and create a different path, a hopeful path forward.

4. Forgiveness is finding ourselves in the wrongdoer—finding our story in their story. It's finding our humanness in theirs and theirs in ours. Forgiveness transcends the wrong and allows us to see the other in our mirror. Forgiveness acknowledges that we're all in this together, that we're more connected than we realize, that the current of forgiveness is for everyone—even the person who caused so much hurt, so much pain, so much sorrow. Because in the end, we're much more alike than we're different and our need for forgiveness is the same as their need for ours.

5. Forgiveness is a choice. That may seem obvious, but if so, why do we often struggle to grant it? Which leads to another question: When has withholding forgiveness, pursuing revenge, and wishing the wrongdoer harm ever made you a more loving, kind, and positive person? Speaking from my own failures, refusing to live in the current of forgiveness leads to a hateful, bitter, and negative mindset, which will never point us toward a more hopeful future.

Let me be clear—

Choosing to forgive will do more to free you from your
self-made prison
than just about any other action you can take in your life.
If gratitude is the bass note of the firm-grip life,
forgiveness is the melody that carries the tune.

Our Own Worst Critic

Several years ago, I was a lay leader in a large church that served our community for three decades. The church was at a crossroads. What brought the church through those decades would not lead the church into its future. Change was needed. Through much work, research, and prayer, the leadership team sought God's direction. As the vision of that direction emerged, we implemented change. Change is always difficult, even more so when a large number of people are involved. Looking back, I see many mistakes we made, the least of which was implementing too much change too quickly and without sufficient communication. The result was the collapse of the church. We held our last service in the fall of 2011.

The church,
as that gathering of people,
was no more.

I accepted great personal responsibility for the closing of a place of worship that had pointed thousands to the Divine for over thirty years. For several years I carried the weight of my failed leadership. I felt responsible to the people I failed, but also to God. This was on me, or so I reasoned. I've no idea how many times I sat in the parking lot of the abandoned, empty shell of the building and wept in my car. I asked God for forgiveness over and over, subconsciously assuming that God would have to work his way through the process of forgiveness too. *This one might take a while,* I thought. Certainly, I wouldn't forgive myself. This would be my cross to bear.

I don't know your past or what you've done that you think is unforgivable, but in my life, I've learned my struggle is more about holding on to the guilt and shame from my actions. Scripture tells us God has removed our sins as far from us as the east is from the west (Psalm 103:12). That's a long way—certainly far enough that if God can forgive me, so can I. But lingering guilt and shame have the same negative effect on us as refusing to forgive ourselves. The Psalmist said,

"Wash me clean from my guilt. Purify me from my sin. For
I recognize my rebellion; it haunts me day and night."
Psalms 51: 2-3 (NLT)

That was my struggle, maybe yours too. When we allow guilt and shame to haunt us day and night, our self-forgiveness is incomplete.

We're declaring the east isn't far enough from the west—that what's good enough for God isn't good enough for us. I let my guilt and shame haunt me for years. But after my diagnosis, and after learning to more freely forgive others, I slowly realized that within the current of forgiveness, there was room to forgive myself as well, to let the guilt and shame go, to offer myself full and complete forgiveness.

The Psalmist also tells us—

> "Finally, I confessed all my sins to you and stopped trying to hide my guilt. I said to myself, I will confess my rebellion to the Lord. And you forgave me! All my guilt is gone." Psalms 32:5 (NLT)

The grace that is the foundation of forgiving others is the same grace that is the foundation of forgiving yourself. The Divine grants you full, complete, and immediate grace-filled forgiveness. He says to you, "We will speak of this no more." He sees no guilt or shame in you because your guilt is in the east and your shame is in the west.

This is why you can forgive yourself!

Rearview Mirror

Does someone else's past have you stuck living in yours? Does your own past haunt you and hold you hostage from moving into a better future? Pursuing the firm-grip life is about creating a new future. Refusing to forgive others or yourself is insisting on living in the past. It's impossible to create a new, positive future when you choose to live in a negative past. The past is in the rearview mirror.

There's nothing to see there. That's not the way you're going. Focus your intentions on forward movements. Forgiving others and yourself allows you to leave your bitterness, resentment, shame, and guilt in the past where they belong.

Shift the way you think about forgiveness. Give yourself space to enter the process. There's a whole new freedom waiting for you when you do, freedom that sheds the negative and leads you into something positive. It may not be easy and it may take a long time, but it starts with a choice. We truly experience firm-grip living when we choose to forgive.

You have the power today,

right now,

to make that choice.

18

Throw it Around Like Confetti

Life Marker: Kindness

Three things in human life are important. The first is to be kind. The second is to be kind. And the third is to be kind.
—Henry James

I met Kim and her four-year-old son Lukas at the assisted living facility where my mom spent the last eighteen months of her life. Kim's uncle also lived there. One day I walked into my mom's apartment to discover Kim and Lukas visiting my mom. Kim told me they met my mom several months earlier in the dining room. Kim said she and Lukas always visited my mom after their visits with Kim's uncle. Because of my mom's dementia, she couldn't remember to tell me about these visits. But soon I noticed handmade cards and gifts left in my mom's apartment. Kim knew my mom would never remember their visits, or that Lukas made gifts for her, but they kept visiting anyway.

Assisted living facilities can be sad, depressing places. Most residents are there until they die or their condition worsens, requiring the next level of care. Many residents don't receive many visitors, even from their own family. I tried to visit mom at least twice per week, but it was hard to see her and the other residents in their age-weary conditions. Yet here was Kim, spending time with her uncle, then my mom, often several times per week. When I asked Kim why they visited mom, she said they just loved her so much and enjoyed sitting and talking with her.

When my mom's health worsened, and she required physical therapy in a facility forty-five minutes away, Kim tracked me down to find out where she could find my mom. She and Lukas continued to visit and Lukas kept making his little gifts for her. When my mom passed away while I was writing this book, Kim showed up at the funeral home and through tear-filled eyes told me how much she would miss my mom.

When my father retired, he found himself with extra time. There were many widows and elderly folks in his church who could no longer drive. My father spent many days each week driving them to doctor appointments, the grocery store, and church each Sunday. He often did odd jobs around their homes and helped with simple repairs. He did this for over 20 years, right up to the time of his death. He was never paid nor expected to be paid, turning down every offer of compensation. He simply wanted to help those who needed help.

My friend Angie works in a Midwest city. Every day, she parks in a designated lot, then walks the remaining few blocks to her office building. Arriving about the same time each day, she noticed she passed the same people on the sidewalk every morning, each in their routine, headed to their workplace. Many walked looking down, avoiding eye contact. Others wore earbuds, consumed in a favorite song or podcast or whatever was streaming into their ears. Angie decided to engage her fellow sidewalk travelers. Each morning Angie was intentional to say hello, forcing eye contact, even if no other response. To those wearing earbuds, she waved to get their attention, offering a kind smile. Over time, her morning companions began to respond, saying hello or good morning. Soon Angie's morning walk was full of smiles and greetings, each eager to see their morning buddies.

When my mom passed away, one of my friends from high school contacted me saying she had a gift for me. Until a recent high school reunion, we hadn't seen each other in decades. We met at the local library where my kind friend gave me two pieces of memorial art she made honoring my mom's life. She told me she wanted to help me always remember my mom. Her art sits in my home, a reminder of my mother's life, but also my friend's kindness.

I've spent a lot of time in gyms over the years. During that time, I've noticed new members are often intimidated, especially if there are a lot of fit people around. I can see it in their eyes and their posture. They just look uncomfortable, like they feel they don't fit in. So, I decided to encourage the newbies. As I walked by, I'd simply say, "I admire your commitment" or "You're doing great," or some similar encouraging words. The response was remarkable—huge smiles followed by something like, "Oh, thank you so much." That simple exchange changed everything for them. The look of fear disappeared, replaced by a new confidence.

The surgery for my cancer occurred in February, the dead of winter in the Midwest. Since we had a three-hour drive to the medical center where I was treated, we were away several days. While gone, a storm dumped several inches of snow. Our driveway is a long incline to our home set back in the woods. As we pulled into our driveway, we discovered it was completely clean. It took several days to learn that a neighbor kept our driveway clear.

There's a group of people in my community who started a center to feed people. It's called The Pax Center (*Pax* is Latin for Peace). Anyone is welcome to attend community meals and shop in The Pax Center's grocery store at no cost. To educate adults and children about healthy nutrition, they built community gardens where folks can plant and harvest, learning the importance of fresh produce as a foundation of healthy nutrition. They refer to the people who use their services as clients or guests, valuing each individual as a fellow human being, created in the image of the Divine. Their goal—simply to love people well.

Heaven on Earth

The world is a harsh place. Every day, we hear of violence, oppression, tragedy, sorrow, and misery. Simple acts of kindness garner little attention. Yet, at its core, there's something about kindness that I'm convinced changes everything, even when we cannot comprehend the full impact kindness has on the world around us. While we may appreciate the benefits of a kind act for the recipient, we underestimate the impact on the giver who offers kindness to another, even when the gesture is simple.

Kindness has a boomerang effect that brings the joy full-circle to the giver of kindness. Think about it—how did you feel the last time you were kind to someone? Even if you had no intent to benefit yourself, being kind made you feel great, didn't it? Your spirit lifted, there was a sense of joy in your heart and you felt uplifted, right? I've come to realize—

It's impossible to be negative when showing kindness to
another person.
Go ahead—read that again.
Impossible.

Kindness carries the potential and propensity to transform
our attitudes because the joy we receive from being kind creates
momentum. Long after the kind act is over, the positive boost
continues. The more acts of kindness we offer, the longer we remain
in a positive state of mind. The longer we maintain a positive mindset,
the more positive our outlook on our lives becomes. Slowly, over
time, we can literally reshape our mental outlook from negative to
positive—simply by being kind to others. While it may seem this leads
to a selfish motivation for being kind, this boomerang effect comes
from the fact that our greatest sense of fulfillment comes from serving
our fellow man.

The Divine wired us for kindness.
Need proof?
Answer this question—
When was the last time you regretted being kind?

If you want to live the firm-grip life, start throwing kindness
around like confetti.

Kind acts need not be monumental. You don't have to quit your
job and go feed kids in a third-world country. You don't have to hand
out $100 bills on the corner. You don't have to start a non-profit
organization.

Simply wake up in the morning and choose to be kind.

Like my friend Angie, just say hello to people you
encounter.
Buy coffee for the person behind you in the drive up.
Let the other driver go even though you were at the
intersection first.
Offer a co-worker a kind word of encouragement.
Tell the clerk at the store he did a great job.
Rake your neighbors' leaves.
Visit an elderly person.
Say thank you more often.
Smile at people you don't know.

It will never be wars or policies or election results or even preachers that change the world. It will be everyday people engaging in acts of kindness that change the world. We can make a difference. We can bring Heaven to Earth. We can be kind and we can love well. We can shine light into dark places through kindness, often to find that the greatest light we shine may be into our own lives. As we light the lives of others, we illuminate our own path and create a new future, a more positive future, a firm-grip life.

Smile, Love and Be Kind

Since my MTC diagnosis, I've become friends with many other MTC warriors who are part of our online support group. They live in countries all around the world as this evil disease knows no boarders and needs no passport. We share our stories, fears and hopes. We talk about our medical care—what worked and what didn't. We encourage each other. We pray for each other. We cry with each other and we mourn together when one of us dies. We've mourned the death of far too many. Just this morning, I attended the funeral of a friend from Minnesota who died from MTC.

He was only thirty-eight.

Emmy Coates was a member of our group. She was a young woman in her early thirties who lived in the United Kingdom. After suffering various symptoms, and being misdiagnosed a couple of times, her doctors diagnosed Emmy with MTC and a short time later told her the cancer had already spread to her lungs, liver, and bones. I've learned that MTC acts differently in each of its hosts, some experiencing rapid metastasis outside the neck while others' cancer seems more well behaved, remaining in the neck region, making treatment much easier with improved prognosis. Emmy was in the group of warriors whose MTC was wild, out of control, and difficult to treat.

Despite her poor prognosis, Emmy always had a smile on her face. Emmy married her childhood friend, and they embarked on an adventure to ride their tandem bike from London to Copenhagen, raising money for The Royal Marsden Cancer Charity to help others fighting various forms of cancer. When asked about her motivation to raise money for cancer patients, Emmy said, "Believe it or not, I am happier than ever. Love is truly the best drug, and I have been totally smothered in it. I am the luckiest lady in the world to be surrounded by so many sensational people." She said, "It is true that you never know what is around the corner. I feel so positive and so blessed and I have never had such a boost to live every day to the full—to smile, to love, and to be kind."

How can she feel blessed when her life is about to be cut short in her early thirties from an evil disease? What drives a person to spend her last months on Earth helping others?

Emmy knew the joy of kindness.

She understood and embraced the truth that kindness helps mend and restore a broken world. And Emmy knew that kindness played a role in the journey to living a positive life narrative... no matter what.

Emmy died at age thirty-one, a year after her marriage, eighteen months after her diagnosis, and only a few short months after raising more than $180,000 to help others fight cancer.

Smile, love, and be kind was Emmy's motto.
She lived that way,
and she died that way.
Emmy lived the firm-grip life,
even if she didn't call it that.

One Day Challenge

Imagine our world if everyone awoke each day with Emmy's motto in their heart, her desire to help others, and a decision to smile, love, and be kind! While it may seem unreasonable to ever expect such a world, I choose to dream big for all things to be restored here on Earth. That could occur if kindness ruled. I believe it's possible. I believe we can create a movement of kindness that could change everything because kindness is a worldwide currency that values everyone equally.

Kindness

has no borders,

knows no limits,

sees past flaws,

doesn't discriminate,

makes no judgments,

cares less about social status,

overlooks political differences,

has no conditions,

expects nothing in return,

and never runs empty.

I'm inviting you to accept a challenge—a challenge to be intentionally kind for one day. To everyone you encounter. No matter who they are, whether you know them and even if you don't like them. One day. Then notice how a day of being kind impacts you, your heart, your soul, your thoughts, your attitude. Be aware of what happens around you and in you. Notice your thoughts and whether they are negative or positive. How should you be kind that day? Well, that is limited only by your imagination.

It's easy to be kind when we have a good day, isn't it? Smiles, high fives, and good vibes are easy to hand out when all is right in our world. But what if kindness still ruled in your world on your bad days? What if you chose to be kind on your worst days when you're surrounded by darkness? Just like Emmy did. I'm confident of this:

being kind to others will improve even your worst of days, change your attitude and help you live the firm-grip life, positive and hopeful. You're wired for kindness and when you live out of kindness toward others, you will experience deep change that will alter your mindset and change the way you live.

I'm suggesting something rather radical here:
Be kind to everyone
all the time—
no matter what.

When someone has wronged you… be kind.
When you're angry… be kind.
When you're frustrated… be kind.
When it feels your world is crashing in around you… be kind.
When you disagree with someone's beliefs, values,
opinions… be kind.
When someone takes advantage of you… be kind.
When you've been treated unkindly… be kind.
When you're offended… be kind.
When all trust has disappeared… be kind.
When you're heartbroken… be kind.
When you're scared… be kind.
When you can be anything…
be
kind.

Kindness, like everything else we've addressed in this book, is a choice. How we treat others is always a choice—no matter our circumstances, no matter theirs. No matter how we feel and no matter how bad our day, week, year, or life is, we always have the power to be kind. We choose it. The world gets better with every act of kindness, even if we can't always see it. Throwing kindness around like confetti improves our lives and the attitude we carry with us into every space we enter.

Do you want to increase your ability to wake up each day and choose to create and live the firm-grip life? Then shift your focus to being intentionally kind to everyone you encounter.

19

Healthy, Fit and Strong

Life Marker: Exercise & Nutrition

This isn't about being skinny or fat; it's about being strong,
confident, and healthy.
—Author Unknown

I grew up active, playing sports, and constantly on the move. As a result, I always had a lean, athletic build. With a fast metabolism and my activity level, I never thought about what I ate—I just seemed to burn it off quickly (I know—lucky, right?). Early adulthood didn't change things much. I played tennis, hockey, and softball, not much interest in sitting around the house.

Then Kids Arrived

Kids change everything. Kids enter our lives and soon we're no longer in charge. They show up, all of maybe six to eight pounds, and the little buggers now run the show. Simple adult functions such as sleeping, eating, and going to work suddenly become monumental tasks. Activities like playing sports become luxuries we can no longer afford because if there's any extra time in our lives, we hope it will be for napping.

As my sons grew, I enjoyed spending time with them. I chose to sacrifice many of my activities to be involved in their lives. Add to that my growing law practice and my time was stretched thin. What I didn't plan on was a slowing metabolism that secretly crept into my life. Over time, I noticed that the numbers on the scale didn't change much, but my waistline was changing and my body shape was shifting. I developed the classic inner-tube-around-my-waist that middle age brings to men. It didn't bother me too much, until the day one of my sons said, "Dad, you're the fattest skinny guy I know."

I joined a gym the following week. I've committed to a fit and healthy lifestyle in the years since then.

Healthy Doesn't Just Happen

We can't control everything about our health. Some are just born with bad genetics and can't do anything about that. I had no control over my body developing cancer. It had nothing to do with my lifestyle, and I did nothing to bring it into my life. It didn't matter how much time I spent in the gym or how healthy I ate, cancer just showed up one day. But I've learned that we have some control over our health, maybe far more than most realize.

We have complete control over the choices we make regarding exercise and nutrition.

Now please don't check out and skip to the next chapter. Hear me out. I have something to say about living fit and healthy that I hope might be a new perspective for you and serve as encouragement, not another guilt trip. But it all starts from this premise:

It's much easier to choose to live the firm-grip life when you feel well.

And you can impact how you feel with the choices you make.

Let's start with a reminder about the health risks of an inactive lifestyle:

- Heart disease
- Obesity
- Type 2 diabetes
- High blood pressure
- Poor circulation
- Joint pain
- Low endurance
- Reduced brain efficiency
- Low self-esteem
- Reduced quality of life

Despite common knowledge of these risks, many of us still fail to make better choices about activity and nutrition. There are as many reasons for this as there are excess pounds on the average adult, but some common reasons include:

- We have an immortality complex.

- We don't think we have the time or energy to exercise.
- We tried before but quit.
- Working out isn't fun.
- We didn't get the results we wanted.
- We view food as entertainment or a reward.

I'm not a certified trainer or nutritionist, but I've learned much about exercise and nutrition that I want to share with you in hope you might shift the way you think about exercise, healthy nutrition, and most importantly, YOU! You might think this shift starts in the gym or the kitchen, but it doesn't. Like most shifts, it starts in your head.

Physical Change Begins with Mental Change

If you're not living a fit and healthy lifestyle, there's a good chance it's not because you haven't tried. You probably have tried— many times—but somewhere along the way gave up. Each time you quit, you felt bad about yourself. Even now, as you read this, those old thoughts and feelings of guilt arise. Negative thoughts swirl in your head as you tell yourself that one of these days you'll get back in the gym and stick with it. Sound familiar?

Negative thoughts don't just accompany a failed attempt to get back in shape, negative thoughts are frequently the reason a person begins a fitness journey. When my son told me I was skinny-fat, a negative image of myself appeared in my head. Think about the reasons you've started a healthy living journey in the past. Chances are you started because of negative thoughts about yourself that might include:

Who will want me if I'm fat?

What will people say at the summer pool parties if I show up with my winter weight?

My waist size is up to WHAT?

I just have to squeeze into that dress for the class reunion, the wedding, or vacation.

Well, I guess the gym is my punishment for "letting myself go."

My family has always been unhealthy.

I hate diets, but now I have no choice.

I'm fat.

Negative—negative—negative!

Negative thoughts might get you to the gym or the produce section in your grocery store, but negative thoughts will rarely sustain a long-term commitment to a healthy lifestyle. That is why most people quit the gym in February after making a New Year's resolution to get in shape—or return to poor eating habits after just a few months of healthier eating. When our motivation is grounded in negative thoughts about ourselves, it's far too easy to quit our health journey when swimsuit season is over or the wedding day has passed. Pursing healthy living on the basis of negative thoughts becomes a grind and makes us feel like we have to go to the gym or eat healthy. Anytime we feel like we "have to do" something, we'll not likely keep doing it for very long.

But what if you shift the way you think about living a
healthy lifestyle?

- What if you pursued a fit and healthy lifestyle, not for him or for her, but for you?
- What if you lived more fit to feel better in your skin rather than your swimsuit?
- What if you changed your thinking from looking good for a special occasion to being healthier for a lifetime?
- What if you chose to live healthier to have more energy and improved confidence?
- What if you lived fit and healthy because you're worthy of feeling great and living your best life?
- And what if you decided you don't have to take care of yourself, but that you get to?

Every—single—day!

Positive—positive—positive!

Although being told I was skinny-fat got me to the gym and away from the cookie aisle, over time I shifted how I thought about my fitness journey and realized it wasn't about how my sons or anyone else saw my waistline, but living fit and healthy was one of the greatest gifts I could give myself physically and mentally. By shifting to a positive approach to my journey, it became easier to maintain a long-term commitment because I was doing it for me—to be the best version of me.

As I began to feel great physically, I noticed an unexpected but welcomed increase in my personal confidence. I was lifting weights, doing calisthenics, and building endurance and stamina through high-intensity interval training, all of which I never could have imagined at middle age. Not arrogance, but an interior pride and confidence arose, causing me to realize I could achieve far more in all aspects of my life than I ever thought possible.

At the time of my MTC diagnosis, I was in the best shape of my life, physically and mentally. Looking back, I'm convinced this was part of a Divine plan. After an eight-hour surgery and a twelve-inch, ear-to-ear incision, my surgeon told me I could return to work slowly—in about a month.

But I had other plans.

I knew the best way for me to not feel like a cancer patient was to return to my normal life as quickly as possible. So that's where I set my intentions. Within a few days of returning home from the hospital, I began the physical return to my life. While confined to my house, I chose to be active. I did arm and leg exercises in my recliner several times a day. I walked laps through my house, finding creative routes around the furniture to expand the distance as much as possible.

Eight days after surgery, I returned to my office for a few hours, even driving myself there. I'd have returned earlier, but I refused to go out in public until the last drain tubes were removed, concerned I'd scare children with my Frankenstein-ish appearance. I was working full-time in two weeks. After begging my surgeon, I returned to low-impact cardio training two weeks after surgery. And after promising my doctor I would "go easy," he allowed me to lift weights and do calisthenics four weeks after surgery.

I'm convinced the only reason I recovered so quickly was my strong physical and mental condition leading into the surgery. If there was ever a test of the benefits of the fit and healthy lifestyle, this was it.

Start Here

So, when you shift your mindset to see a healthy lifestyle as a positive, enjoyable way to live, how can you channel your positive mindset into a sustainable fitness journey that will radically improve your life physically and mentally and help you create a positive, firm-grip life? Here are a few tips to consider—

1. Find an activity that's fun. I've seen people grind out sessions on a treadmill day after day. When they disappear from the gym, I'm never surprised. Unless you love treadmills, they're not much fun. So, it's important you find an exercise you enjoy. Whether it's running, biking, swimming, lifting weights, playing tennis, yoga, whatever you choose, make sure you enjoy it. The more you enjoy the activity, the more likely you'll continue to exercise.

2. Switch up your routine. No matter how much you enjoy a particular activity, you'll benefit from varying your exercises. Trying new activities is fun and keeps your training interesting and prevents boredom. You'll meet new people, like-minded about healthy living as you experiment with different activities, creating a broader support network. Changing up your routines periodically also helps prevent homeostasis, the process by which your body adapts to training, producing decreased results. When you perform a variety

of exercises, you keep your body guessing and force it to continue to adapt, resulting in a healthier and stronger you.

3. Set short-term, achievable goals. If your long-term goal is to lose one hundred pounds, you'll struggle to remain committed if all you focus on is that one hundred pounds because it will take a long time to accomplish. But if you focus on losing five pounds, you can and will achieve that goal repeatedly, gaining momentum and encouragement along the way, both of which are crucial to remaining dedicated to living fit and healthy for a lifetime. Setting achievable goals also keeps you competitive with yourself and provides a target to shoot for.

4. Focus on non-scale victories. Too much focus in fitness is on weight rather than health. The scale only gives you a number. It can't tell you how much healthier you've become. It won't tell you how much lean muscle you've gained, lean muscle which, by the way, weighs more than fat. The scale won't report the increased endurance you've gained or how much farther you can now walk, run, or bike. The scale, unlike a mirror, won't show you how your body composition has changed, or how your clothes fit more loosely. The scale can't tell you how much self-confidence you've gained. The scale is only a number—and you are far more than a number!

5. Remain consistent. In the fit and healthy lifestyle, I always say consistency is king. Nothing will deliver better results than staying consistent with your workouts and nutrition. Make a weekly plan for when and how often you'll exercise—then stick to it. Make your workout sessions a priority in your life just like going to work, keeping

important appointments, and spending time with family and friends. Your health is important because you've made the decision that you are worthy of self-care. After all, we all find time for what is really important to us, don't we?

6. Celebrate every success. There is no end-game or destination in the fit and healthy lifestyle. There is only the journey which lasts a lifetime. So, every time you achieve a goal, accomplish a personal best, lift a heavier weight, walk a faster lap, swim farther, run another quarter mile, finally pick up those intimidating dumbbells—every time you make yourself smile over what you just did—celebrate that! There may be many others on the fitness journey, but this one is yours, so be very proud of yourself for everything you accomplish.

7. Include resistance training. Male or female, no matter what type of exercise you choose, always include some form of resistance training such as cable-weight machines, free weights, calisthenics, or resistance bands. An important part of living fit and healthy is strength. As we age, our muscles decline. The only way to maintain or increase muscle is to force your muscles to work harder, which generates muscle growth.

8. Consider high-intensity interval training (HIIT). HIIT is a type of cardio that includes short intervals of intense exertion followed by a period of recovery. For example, I perform HIIT on my elliptical trainer where I expend maximum effort for thirty seconds followed by forty-five to sixty seconds of slowed pace, moving just enough to keep the machine going while I recover for the next thirty-second, high-intensity interval. I repeat this cycle for fifteen to twenty

minutes. You can perform HIIT on any cardio machine, or many other ways, only limited by your imagination: sprints followed by a walk back to the start line, high knees, jumping rope, box jumps, and more. HIIT burns calories for up to twenty-four hours after completion compared to steady-state cardio that has a maximum calorie burn of two hours after completion. And HIIT accomplishes that in shorter cardio sessions.

9. Love yourself now while striving to improve. Don't wait to love yourself until you've lost weight, or can walk a mile, or ride your bike around the block, or reached your goal. Don't tell yourself you'll be worthy when someone else notices your hard work and results. You're doing this for yourself because you decided you're worth the effort. That means you are of immense value already, where you are and who you are—today. You're not pursuing a healthy lifestyle to become worthy—you're already worthy! You're pursuing a healthy lifestyle simply to be better, to create a daily best version of yourself. Today, you are your current best you. Love that person!

10. Understand the importance of rest. Our bodies need rest—on average, seven to eight hours of sleep each night. Rest is even more important when you're living an active lifestyle. It's during rest that our bodies repair, getting healthier and stronger from our hard work. So just as you plan your work-week and now your training schedule, plan for rest. Build it into your schedule like all your other important commitments.

Exercise shouldn't be something to dread. If you're doing activities you enjoy, and having fun, you'll always feel good about yourself, knowing you're taking care of the one and only body you'll ever have.

Remember, we don't get a do-over at the end of our lives.

Fuel

Several years ago, I attended a reception to welcome a new Indiana Supreme Court Justice to the bench. As I spoke with the Justice and another attorney, the conversation turned to exercise and nutrition. The Justice was also a fitness enthusiast. The other attorney remarked that he worked out so he could eat whatever he wanted. As if the lawyer had just made an inappropriate remark in the courtroom, this Supreme Court Justice barked at him that his statement was the most ridiculous thing he'd ever heard. Fifteen minutes later, the attorney had received a judicial lesson about the importance of both exercise and nutrition to achieve a healthy life.

Like the Justice, I don't believe we can live a fully fit and healthy lifestyle without proper nutrition. But I think we place too much emphasis on the number of calories we consume, rather than the quality of the calories we consume. Our cars perform best when we fuel them with quality gasoline. Our bodies are no different. Food is fuel for the body. The higher quality fuel we give our bodies, the better they'll perform. I also believe healthy nutrition is much easier than we realize.

I propose four points to consider about nutrition:

1. Food fuels our metabolism. Our metabolism controls how quickly our bodies burn calories. Regardless of what any diet promises about weight loss, a calorie deficit is the only way to lose weight—you have to burn more calories than consumed. The faster your metabolism, the more calories you burn. But your metabolism works, in part, based on the fuel you put in your body so to keep your metabolism going, you need to eat. When we deny our body food, as happens with many diets, the metabolism slows, resulting in fewer calories burned. Fewer calories burned means reduced opportunity for caloric deficit, resulting in less weight loss. A great place to start is to learn your basil metabolic rate (BMR). You can find BMR calculators online.

2. I don't believe in diets. The vast majority of diets are not sustainable for a lifetime as they come with far too many restrictions. Who wants to count points for every meal of every day for the rest of your life? Who wants to carry around a cooler containing the foods purchased from the people who created the diet? Who wants to replace a meal with a shake made with powder and water? These plans might work for a short time and result in rapid weight loss, but once the unrealistic nature of the diet long-term sets in, the diet is usually abandoned, and the person returns to old eating patterns and they regain the weight in a short time. Diets typically leave people feeling hungry, irritable, and negative.

3. Eat whole foods. Our Creator provided all the healthy fuel we need. We can achieve healthy nutrition by consuming whole foods. Don't buy into the latest fad diet or weight loss plan. You don't have to starve yourself, nor do you have to eat foods you don't like. Our

bodies require quality calories for daily living and to recover from workouts. You can find great lists of healthy, whole foods online, but here's a short list to get you started:

> **Lean proteins**: Poultry, fish, beans, eggs, bison, Greek yogurt, tofu, lean beef, nuts.
>
> **Complex Carbohydrates**: Vegetables, oats, whole grains, quinoa, sweet potatoes, fruit, brown rice.
>
> **Healthy Fats**: Avocados, olive oil, seeds, nuts, salmon, coconut oil, dark chocolate.

4. Follow the 80/20 rule. I try my best to eat quality nutrition eighty percent of the time. That means the other twenty percent, I'm free to indulge a little. Eat the cake! Have the ice cream! Go on, enjoy that warm chocolate chip cookie! To live fit and healthy doesn't mean you can't enjoy sweets and treats. What fun is life if we're always depriving ourselves of the joys of the palate? Here's the great thing— when you follow this rule, you don't have to feel guilty or like you're cheating when you slam some tasty treats.

Fit for Life

I was working out at a beach in Naples, Florida a couple years ago, running sand sprints, when a lady asked me, "What are you training for?" "Life," I responded. It's really that simple. It's about embracing the bodies we've been given, moving to keep them working well, and fueling with quality foods as much as possible.

Living a fit and healthy life is both a gift to ourselves and to those who love us and want us to stick around this planet for a while longer.

The good thing is that it's never too late, and you're never too old to start. Sure, you might not run a marathon, or even have the desire to, but you can always find fun ways to move your body regularly to improve your health and increase your self-confidence. As I say often, I'm not looking to add days to my life, but life to my days.

You don't have to live fit and healthy to create a positive-focused, firm-grip life, but why wouldn't you want to? Smart nutrition and exercise can significantly improve the way you feel physically and mentally. Those improvements add to the joy of life and help eliminate health problems that would otherwise drag you into negativity.

You have the power to shift the way you think about
exercise and healthy nutrition.
You can change your view of exercise
to something you get to do
because you're worth it.

20

Day Seven

Life Marker: Rest

Instead of wondering when your next vacation is, maybe you should set up a life you don't need to escape from.
—Seth Godin

Jane and I were in our mid-twenties when we bought our first home. I was still in law school and she was a recent college graduate so our budget was slim. Most mid-level new cars today cost what we paid for that home. But we were young, full of excitement, and ready for opportunity.

It was an older home with older home problems. One of those problems was the galvanized pipes, clogged and corroded from decades of use. This problem was most obvious when taking a shower, the water gathering around our feet, the drain unable to keep up with the water flow. Over time, the water around our feet became the water above our ankles and Jane urged me to do something before it became the water at our knees.

Off to the hardware store, I bought a drain snake. To my dismay, after several excursions into the nether regions of our pipes, the problem didn't resolve. Hoping to avoid the expense of a plumber, and with the determination of a first-time homeowner set on being king of my castle, I ventured back to the hardware store. A store clerk handed me a tall, shiny can resembling a can of spray paint, but this can was full of compressed air.

Armed with modern technology I was certain would cure our water woes, I headed home, eager to prove to Jane that I was indeed her handyman and could handle a simple clogged drain. Although men rarely need to read instructions, I read just enough to confirm that I already knew how to work this can of magic. I blocked other vents in the bathroom drain system as instructed, leaving open only the sink drain to relieve excess pressure and avoid pipe damage.

Turning the can upside down and placing the domed top into the drain, with the eagerness of a kid on Christmas morning, I pushed down, releasing a powerful blast of air. Nothing. More determined than ever, I laid into the can, blasting a long stream of oxygenated plumbing expertise into the bowels of my home. Within seconds I heard high-pressure air escaping like from a boiling teapot, but then I heard the sound of something splattering, followed by something smacking against my back.

The open sink drain was a volcano erupting black lava everywhere—walls, ceiling, curtains, window, door, floor, and even the hallway carpeting. The lava was a thick, black, greasy, smelly, disgusting combination of decades of soap, hair, body grime, deteriorated pipe innards, and whatever else had managed its way into those pipes. I had the stinking slime all over me, launching a full-blown gagging session.

Desperate to keep this toxic catastrophe a secret from Jane, I did what most independent, multi-skilled men (who need not read *all* the directions) do—I called my mom, who arrived on the disaster scene quickly. After hours of scrubbing, we restored our home to a livable environment. Despite my mom's best life-saving efforts, the curtains and floor rugs succumbed to their injuries, and a large stain remained in the hallway carpeting, resembling an outline of a death that had just occurred. I had no choice but to tell Jane that I almost turned our house into an unlivable, toxic waste site. She was quick to forgive and laughed as I described what happened.

The worst part?
The problem wasn't resolved, and I still had to pay a
plumber to fix it.

Our lives are often like my bathroom pipes—packed with pressure until something blows, creating a massive mess to clean up. Our generation lives the most fast-paced lives humankind has ever experienced. Like I forced air into every inch of my pipes, we pack every space in our lives with activity—work, church, social life, clubs and organizations, boards, committees, year-round kid's sports, community involvement—until there's no space left. We get up in the morning stressed over today's schedule and go to bed at night anxious about tomorrows. And when the pressure becomes too much, our lives erupt like my bathroom pipes, resulting in broken relationships, health problems, stress, substance abuse, and many other forms of ruin; some, like the stain in my carpet, permanent.

Crazy-Busy

We live in a culture that values productivity above all else. From the time we wake in the morning until we drag our weary bodies to bed at night, we're driven to produce at work, around our homes, in our finances, in relationships, and all the other commitments we make. We live under constant pressure to do more, produce more, advance more, stretch ourselves more, be more available, and give of ourselves more.

- Eight-hour workdays seldom produce what is expected, so we work longer hours than any other generation in history.

- I know people who speak of long, seven-day work weeks as if giving their lives away to a job is a badge of honor or status symbol.

- I know stay-at-home moms so busy they hire others to clean their house.

- I've known pastors who spent so much time preparing for sermons, visiting people in the hospital, performing weddings and funerals, leading week-night activities and caring for the needs of the church that they neglected their own family.

- Jane and I spent almost every summer weekend taking our sons to travel baseball tournaments.

- We all carry pocket-sized computers that keep us connected to people and obligations 24/7. Handy? Sure. Healthy? Probably not.

We're obsessed with being busy, even when the pace of our lives is completely out of control. We feel guilty when we're not productive, as if we're wasting time. When asked how we are, the standard answer is now, "Crazy-busy," as if any other answer would make us less successful, less driven, less valued, less worthy.

How did crazy-busy become a good thing?
When did our worth,
as viewed by others or ourselves,
depend on how productive we are?

When the measuring stick of our self-worth is based on our level of productivity, we can never rest because we can always produce more. Periodically, we notice the craziness of our schedules and the pace of our lives. We realize we need a break, so we go on vacation or a weekend get-away to slow the pace, to catch our breath, to hit the reset button.

Remember when you came back from that vacation and
had new perspectives on life?
On priorities?
On what really matters?
Remember thinking there's more to life than the one you
were living before you caught your breath again?
Remember committing to keep that new perspective so life
would be slower and lived more fully?
How long did that last after you returned to your normal
schedule?
Did you even make it a week?

Often, the means by which we attempt to regain control of our lives and ease the pressure of crazy-busy schedules is temporary, like opening a vent in my pipe system to release air. When we return to our fast-paced lives, it's like stuffing rags back into the drain vents, a disastrous explosion just waiting to blow.

- But what if you could permanently slow the pace of your life?
- What if you could wake each day to a life that isn't pressure-packed and filled with more expectations than you can meet?
- What if you could be guilt-free when you aren't producing?
- What if you could control your schedule rather than your schedule controlling you?

The firm-grip life is about learning to live at a pace and within rhythms you were designed to live. It's possible. But you'll need to shift the way you think and make some new choices.

Cancer, Creation, and Gold Medals

I've lived a pace of life that was unhealthy, unrealistic, and unsustainable. I excused my fast-paced lifestyle on being motivated, driven, determined to make my mark, make my wealth, help people, and give back to my community. My schedule was pressure-packed with many good things. Few would say my motivations were bad. But I realized I couldn't maintain this pace. I knew I would burn out or, worse, explode like my bathroom pipes. With new perspectives that slowly arrived with age, I was already re-thinking and re-shaping my priorities and slowing my pace when cancer showed up.

When I was diagnosed, I couldn't maintain the fast-paced life I was living—not because of physical issues, but because of the mental real estate the diagnosis consumed. I went from a daily agenda filled with commitments to a single-track agenda—figuring out a way to survive. My mind didn't have near enough bandwidth to deal with much more than the cancer and my desire to stay alive. My focus narrowed and was entirely priority-driven—faith, family, and friends. Sure, I kept working, but I protected my schedule to permit only my highest priorities to occupy space in my life. Cancer forced me into a new life rhythm where priorities were more than just cliché but were truly what I pursued.

> There were no longer blurred lines between what was
> important and what wasn't.
> Life slowed down.

This allowed me to realize how consumed I'd been with busyness, how much pressure busyness had created in my life, how my fast-paced, busyness-driven life had controlled me. It was clear I'd been a slave to being busy, believing all along this was normal—just the way life was. With a slower pace, I realized my busyness had kept my mind so occupied that I rarely lived in a single... present... moment. I was always living in moments yet to arrive, focused on what I needed to accomplish next. Even when I had free time, I always thought about my "should do" list.

Most importantly, I learned that living crazy-busy isn't a
scheduling problem—
it's a soul problem.
Crazy-busy is outside of God's design for how we are to
live.

There's an ancient poem we visited in chapter ten that tells the
creation story. In this poem, we're told the Divine spent six days
creating. In those early days, God was quite busy, creating Heaven
and Earth, light and dark, land and sea, sun and moon, plants and
animals. On the sixth day in this poem, found in Genesis 1, God made
humans, bearing his image, reflecting the very nature of God and God
blessed them.

We, humans, were made by,
and blessed by,
the Creator of all things.
Those were a very busy six days.

But this poem is a seven-day poem that spills over into Genesis
2, where we learn that after God worked and created, down to
every detail, on the seventh day, God rested. God, who worked and
accomplished and created more in six days than all of humanity for all
time will ever create, rested.

The creation story doesn't end with work—it ends with
rest.
Rest was not an add-on or less important than the six days
when God was working.

Rest was part of the creation process.
The creation story would be incomplete without rest on
day seven.
The seventh day is part of the story,
part of our story,
part of who we are,
and how we're to live.

There's a rhythm to creation. All creation is designed around the rhythms of work and rest. The days give us light to work while the night gives us darkness to rest. It happens every twenty-four hours—in rhythm. The seasons come and go in a rhythmic pattern of planting and tending, then harvest, followed by the Earth resting and restoring to prepare for another season; that will come in its time to start the process all over again.

Spring, summer, fall, winter—in rhythm.

We're part of creation. So, there is to be a rhythm in us, just like our rhythm of inhaling and exhaling, the essence of life. God, who made us in his image, rested. Our life is to reflect the rhythms of work and rest as those who carry the DNA of the Divine.

Crazy-busy is a six-day poem.
Crazy-busy doesn't rest.
Crazy-busy doesn't know a seventh day.
But we were Divinely created to live
and move
and breathe
within a seven-day poem.

When we live outside the rhythms in which we were created to live, we dismiss the image and reflection of the Divine within us. When we live as if the poem has only six days, our life feels unsettled, disconnected, off balance, and out of rhythm. But those feelings are simply the urgings of the Divine to reorient our lives to the rhythms we were created for, calling us back to rest, reminding us to embrace the seventh day, to live out the full image of the Divine within us.

What does it look like to return to creation's rhythms for
work and rest?
How do we slow our lives,
reduce our pace
and reconnect
with the rhythms
we were designed for?

Usain Bolt was a Jamaican sprinter. He won nine gold medals over three consecutive Olympics. He's widely considered the greatest sprinter of all time and was labeled the fastest man on Earth. I know little about track and have never had much interest in the sport. But when the Olympics were on television, I always watched the races Bolt ran. It was never really a question of whether he'd win, but how badly he'd beat his opponents.

Bolt only ran three events. I always thought if I was the coach and had a runner like Bolt, I'd have him run every event and win every race. But at the world's highest level of competition, it doesn't work that way. Bolt had to pick what he knew he was best at and focus his efforts and training on winning those events. He probably could have been good in every event, but he knew he could be the best at those three.

God also uniquely created you with certain talents and passions. Like Bolt, there may be many events you could be good at, but you know there are certain events you're best at. It's easy to get caught up in trying to run all the races, isn't it? We know we can't win them all, but we have a hard time saying no, so we sign on for too many races. We run them all, try our best, but fail to perform our best—not even in our best events.

How often do you pursue the good at the expense of your best?
How often do you do many things, but none of them well?
What if you had the courage to say no to all the races
so, you can focus your efforts on your best races?

The first step in slowing down and creating space for rest is not about saying no, but about saying yes—yes, to those things you were created for. If you look at what's got you crazy-busy, there are probably a lot of very good things on your schedule. But just because they are good does not mean you should pursue them.

So how do you know what you're best at?
How do you know what your "yeses" are?

Oh, you know.

Your yeses…
stir your soul,
make you excited to get up in the morning,

> give you purpose and meaning,
> draw out the best in you,
> give you a positive focus,
> and make you feel alive.

These are your "yeses"—your gold medal events. Gold medals are what the Divine wired you for. Gold medals are what you should pursue. There's nothing wrong with silver and bronze medals. In fact, what's silver and bronze to you will be someone's else's gold. But let's face it—even made in the image of the Divine, we can only do a few things well. If you struggle to identify your "yeses" because your senses have been dulled by running every race you thought you had to run, spend some time with your trusted tribe, those who know you best, sometimes better than you may know yourself. Ask them to help you once again see your gold medal events. Once you discover them, it's easy to say no to those things that distract you from pursuing your "yeses." And when you can finally say no, you begin to let go of crazy-busy and you create space for rest.

Many traditions refer to the seventh day of rest as Sabbath, a day set aside by the Divine as a Holy day, a day to rest from work and restore our bodies and souls, to connect with the Divine. When you stop chasing medals that aren't yours to chase, you invite Sabbath back into your life, rest that is created just for you, by the One who knows what you need. You also free your life from a pace that is unhealthy and unsustainable. Slowing our pace and restoring the rhythms of rest slows our interior life as well, inviting us to be present in our moments, quieting our soul to hear the voice of the Divine, and opening us to awareness of God's intentions in and through our lives.

Cancer forced me to slow down, examine my life rhythms, and make new choices. When we suffer our darkest days yet choose to rise, we emerge with new perspectives earned in the struggle. Those perspectives form the foundations for shifts in our thinking and lead to our ability to make new choices to create a more positive-focused future. I'm not sure what your dark days brought to you, but I'm certain that along with pain and fear, your darkness also brought you opportunities to embrace new perspectives, new ways of thinking, and opportunities to make new choices.

Are you living crazy-busy?
Exhausted, unsettled and disconnected?

You don't have to live that way. There's a day seven, and it was created for you. You can choose the firm-grip life and free yourself from the crazy-busy pace of life you've been living.

You

can

rest.

Living a life of crazy-busy is a choice.
Taking your life back from crazy-busy
is also a choice.

PART III

Creating Your Firm-Grip Life

21

Here, Not There

_____

The unaware life is not worth living.
—Socrates

Several years ago, a guy walked into a nearby car dealership claiming to be me and tried to get a key made for my car. He knew my name and address, my vehicle identification number, and that I'd purchased my car from that dealership. When the employee asked for identification, the guy left. That alert employee notified me immediately. Jane and I wondered who this guy was and whether he had any plans more sinister than stealing my car. After a few restless nights, concerned this individual might break in, we installed a home security system.

The system includes sirens inside and outside our home; it also notifies local law enforcement if the system isn't deactivated within a short interval after the alarm is triggered. Originally, the alarm was programmed to trip when the phone line went dead. Since our home is in the woods, we lost our phone service frequently to falling branches taking out the lines. It was particularly startling when it happened in the middle of the night. I remember nights being awakened from deep sleep by the shrill blast of the screeching sirens. Startled, I flew out of bed, dazed and half asleep, and ran down the stairs to deactivate the alarm before the interval elapsed. It was not until after I deactivated the alarm that I became alert, fully awake, got my bearings and could think clearly. With increased clarity came the realization that I could have run down those stairs and right into an intruder. I functioned as a person physically awake, but mentally still asleep, just going through the motions of something that had become familiar.

We live our lives that way much of the time. We become so familiar with our schedules, the people around us, and our routines, we set life on autopilot, go through the motions, and get through our days. We function physically awake but mentally asleep to what is going on in and around us. We become robotic in our thoughts and actions. As a result, we lose our sense of awareness, living unconnected to the moment, and the people around us.

We're running down the stairs as fast as possible,
but we aren't really aware of what is happening
right in front of us.

There, Not Here

Have you ever read an entire page of a book, getting to the bottom only to realize that though you read every word, you had no idea what you just read, your mind far away?

Have you ever driven to a destination, only to realize after you arrived that you had no recollection of the actual drive itself? You had no recollection of your turns, stops, and movements on the road, yet somehow you ended up right where you intended. You were physically present but your mind was far away, consumed by the day ahead, your next appointment, a work project, an earlier argument with your kid or any of a million other things occupying your headspace.

Have you ever told yourself you'll truly be happy when…

The weekend arrives?

You finally get married?

You land that great job?

You have a family?

You make more money?

You buy that big house?

You have financial security?

You can finally retire?

You live in constant expectation of a "someday," longing for it to arrive, dismissing all your "todays" as if they don't matter. In the meantime, you're driving through the days of your life, unable to recall the turns, the stops, and losing track of the life you're living today. You're always thinking about, wishing for, waiting to get… there. Always distracted by what's *next*, you're unable to see what's *here*… right in front of you.

You're there.

Not here.

When we're always there not here, we aren't present in this moment, the one that is happening right now, the only moment we truly have. And when we aren't present in this moment, we're unaware of everything this moment offers. There is always more going on in this moment than the obvious, but you have to be aware to see it, to appreciate it, to experience it. Awareness is about expanding your consciousness, being mindful, waking up to see what you've not noticed before, yet has likely been there all along. It's about realizing there's so much more going on in and around you than you've ever imagined. But you have to be awake… in this moment… now.

I've learned that living the firm-grip helps me live here not there.

There is power in the moments of our lives. That power comes in many forms:

- recognition of the good that exists in your life—right now.
- deep appreciation for the people in your tribe—every day.
- the realization you're connected to everything and everyone around you—all the time.
- perceiving the presence of the Divine in your life—in every single moment.

What if you could live each day fully aware of those and other powerful awakenings?
I know.
It seems too good to be true to be able live that way, doesn't it?
Maybe that's because you've been *there* too long.
Maybe it's time for you to be *here*.

Learning to Live Here

A small plaque in our house says, "Be aware of the little things for one day you will realize they were the big things." Dark and difficult times have a way of becoming that "one day" and often wake us, create new awareness, give us new eyes to see through a different lens, and grant us the ability to be *here*.

After my diagnosis, I was suddenly aware of the little things—the pure joy of being home with my family for an evening and doing nothing but being together, sitting with my elderly mother, and seeing the joy on her face as she told stories of her childhood, taking a bike ride or a walk on a sunny day with Jane, a friend stopping by for a visit. These little things happened frequently before my diagnosis. But they became the big things after the darkness visited my life. I realized I'd spent too much time *there*. Now I was *here*—awake, aware, recognizing the beauty of the present moment right in front of me and in each little thing.

Is it possible that the darkness that invaded your life might be your middle-of-the-night, screeching alarm? To awaken you to your life, how you're living, and the choices you make? Of the beauty that exists—that was really there all along, but for which you just didn't have eyes to see? When we choose to rise from our pain, grief, chaos, and all that came from living through horrific times—when we choose to accept it for what it is and allow our pain to become our teacher, we create the opportunity to live an awakened life. Because difficult times rarely come without offering the gift of new eyes to see. We just have to accept the gift.

In Part II of this book, we looked at life markers in which we make daily choices that impact our mental attitude toward life. If you're planning to make a serious run at living the firm-grip life, shifting the way you think, and making new choices to create and live a more positive-focused life, as discussed in those chapters, you must awaken, become aware, and live here… now…this moment.

Living awake and aware in the present moment is the only
way to truly....

- make gratitude the bass note of your life.
- kick fear and worry to the backseat by listening to truth rather than the lies they tell you.
- value your own uniqueness and stop comparing yourself to others.
- break the habit of complaining and avoid the negativity that follows.
- live as your true self and make your greatest contribution to the world as you.
- understand that less can be so much more.
- create a future that doesn't hold us captive to our finances.
- offer grace instead of judgment.
- value the sacredness in the relationships of your tribe.
- realize that forgiveness is the path to escape the hauntings of your past and free yourself.
- understand that being generous with kindness will change the world and you.
- appreciate the positive impact exercise and healthy nutrition have on your body and mind.
- embrace the joy of the life rhythms offered in the rest of day seven.

We have to live connected to each moment to be aware of our words, thoughts, and actions. And only when we live in that connection can we know what new choices are necessary to refocus our lives back to all that it means to live the firm-grip life. If this book has encouraged you to shift your thinking and make new choices that create the firm-grip life, you must take your life off autopilot and live connected to what is happening in and around you. If you don't, you'll continue to live in your old default patterns and choices, and you'll keep running down the stairs as fast as you can, but asleep to all the opportunities to the change you seek. You have to stop living *there*… and start living *here*.

Living *here* is a discipline, just like practicing intentional gratitude or exercising. And like any other discipline, it takes time and intention to live awake and aware. Mindful living requires a conscious decision to awaken to what is happening all around you. It takes time to develop the daily habits and practices needed. Below are some strategies that help keep me living awake and aware and being present.

1. Start each day with a centering practice. I begin most mornings exercising, then reading scripture and connecting with the Divine. When my days begin connected to the source of my being, recognizing the gift of my life, seeing the hand of God working in and through me and knowing that I'm immeasurably loved by a God I can trust with everything I have and all that I am, I'm flooded with peace and calm. Worrisome thoughts that would force me to live *there* are removed because I center my mind and heart in what matters—a trusting knowledge that my life is where it's supposed to be right now, in this very moment. When I'm centered in my connectedness to the Divine, I'm aware and awake. Starting my day *here* helps keep me awake and focused on the moment in front of me throughout the day.

Find your daily centering practice. It could be meditation, yoga, prayer, breathing exercises, reading a book, or listening to music.

Whatever it is, engage a daily practice that centers your soul at the beginning of your day, brings you to a place of peace, and awakens you to what is right in front of you *here*. Starting your day in that place of calm and presence will make it easier to stay connected to the present moments in your day.

2. Maintain perspective. No matter how positively focused we live, darkness will creep in, problems will arise, and daily struggles and irritations always exist. Without intentionally controlling our response, these problems will jettison us to living *there*. Most of our problems ultimately resolve themselves without catastrophic consequences in our lives. But without being intentional about keeping healthy perspectives, we'll allow our thoughts to consume us, convinced of the cataclysmic downfall that awaits us. Worry is always about living *there* not *here*. When daily struggles tempt me to live *there*, I ask myself, "*Will this concern still exist a year from now, a month, a week, even tomorrow?*" This practice helps me maintain perspective and stay in the present moment.

3. Listen to the words you speak to others, and the words you speak to yourself. Our words matter far more than we realize. Words create energy, positive or negative.

I encourage you to be intentional about listening to yourself as you engage conversations with others. What type of energy do your words generate? Are you offering hope, encouragement and positivity, or are you speaking negative energy into the lives of others? Are you taking part in negative conversations, complaining about circumstances, and speaking words of judgment of others?

Just as important, what kind of energy do you create in your life with the words you speak to yourself? Listening to your own words creates awareness, awakens you to your attitude and the posture of your soul, and places you right in the middle of the present moment *here*. That awareness creates opportunity, when needed, to change your words, thoughts, and attitudes to create positive energy.

4. Practice the presence of the Divine. There's a story in Genesis 28 in which Jacob stops for the night to sleep. Using a stone for a pillow, Jacob has a dream and God appears and tells him he'll be blessed, and all people on Earth will be blessed through his descendants, and that God was giving him the very land on which he slept. Jacob awoke the next morning proclaiming that God was in that very place, and he'd been unaware of it. Likewise, Moses stood before the burning bush, hearing God say to remove his shoes because Moses was unaware the ground where he stood was Holy.

Living awake and aware is about being grounded in the here and now and understanding that there is something much larger happening in and around us than what's obvious. We are deeply connected to the Divine in every single moment, in every place we find ourselves. Richard Rohr said, "We cannot attain the presence of God because we are already totally in the presence of God. What's absent is awareness."[1]

We live in a physical world, yet I'm convinced we simultaneously exist in a spiritual realm that is all around us, all the time, and at its center is the very presence of God. Living awake and aware takes us to this presence, allowing us to experience this Divine presence even in the ordinary and mundane—while we take out the trash, mow the lawn, or drive to work. Be intentional about momentary connections with God throughout your day. Whisper a short prayer at work, offer a gesture of adoration, ask for grace in your interactions with others. See the Divine in everything; your pet, a field of crops, the people walking past your house, or the horizon in front of you. Hear the Spirit in the wind. Give thanks for the current moment, who you're with and the task before you. See the burning bushes all around you, all the time, for in every moment, you're standing on Holy ground. Practicing the presence of God in your life will increase your ability to live an awakened life.

5. Check in with yourself several times a day. In our home, we've always had an understanding that we'll let each other know where we are. We stay in touch, send a text when we've arrived at our destination. We always told our sons to tell us if their plans changed, and they would be somewhere other than their original destination. As our sons have become adults, we still all check in periodically, so we know where everyone is. Just today, Jane checked in to let me know her plane landed.

I've developed a practice of checking in with myself several times a day to see where I am. Am I *here* or *there*? What are my attitudes? What are my thoughts? What kind of energy am I putting out? What kind of energy am I creating within? Am I thinking, acting, speaking, and living a positive, firm-grip vibe? Or have I defaulted to old patterns of thought and action that lead to a negative vibe? Checking in with myself increases my awareness and helps me make attitude adjustments to get back on track to the firm-grip life. This practice helps me develop a mindful self-awareness of what is happening, not just around me, but in me.

Checking in with yourself will help you get back to living *here* not *there*. But it takes time to develop a practice of checking in with yourself throughout the day. Most of us are simply not accustomed to such a practice. It might be helpful to set a reminder on your phone, place a note on your computer screen, in your car, and on your bathroom mirror. You can even schedule it on your calendar with an entry that says, *"Hey you! Where are you?"* Hopefully over time, your answer will be, *"I'm right here!"*

Living awakened and aware is a core foundation to creating and living the firm-grip life. Self-awareness is an awaking of the soul that keeps you connected to your interior life and points you to the shifts you need to make in the way you think and the choices you need to make to get you on track (or back on track) to living the way you desire—the positive-focused, firm-grip life.

So, surrender your thoughts to the present moment, to what's happening in and around you right now, being aware of the wonder and awe of THIS moment HERE.

You have this moment.

Do something spectacular with it

by simply being present to it,

alive,

awake

and aware.

22

Old Boards and Copper Nails

If you hear a voice within you say, "You cannot paint," then
by all means paint and that voice will be silenced.
—Vincent van Gogh

When I was a kid, I loved to pound nails into boards. Oddly, I only did this at my grandmother's house. But I was there a lot. Sometimes I'd sit for hours, hammer in hand, banging away. My grandmother bought nails just so I could pound them into old pieces of wood because I'd gone through all the old jars of nails leftover from when my grandfather was alive. It's hard to explain, but to this day, there's something peaceful for me in feeling the weight of the hammer slowly work the metal spike into the wood, just enough tension from the wood pushing back through the hammer into my hand. I've met people who feel the same about hand-sawing wood. We're an odd lot.

There came a time when my grandmother's health no longer permitted her to live in her home. I was then well into my twenties and had long since stopped pounding nails into boards. After she moved to a nursing home, I helped my dad prepare her house for sale.

She was from a generation that knew poverty, so she kept everything, thinking the day might come when each item would be useful.

One evening I was working my way through a pile of old garage items, my dad encouraging me to discard as much as possible. I found a tarp, bulging over what laid beneath. Pulling the tarp away, I discovered a large pile of old boards, each one jammed full of nails that a little boy had pounded in years earlier. I stood in silence, staring at those boards—far too many to count. "Grandma kept my boards," I whispered aloud to myself. In an instant, I was back on her front porch, hammer in hand, tiny fingers squeezing a small nail I was about to hammer into some old piece of wood. It reminded me of how much my grandma loved me, and I her.

Which leads again to my son, Adam.

Adam is a very talented artist. I don't think he realizes that yet, but it's true. In his early teens, he'd sit for hours sketching in a book, drawing pictures from what he saw in his mind. I was always amazed how quickly and beautifully he could sketch whatever he saw. I often wished I could get into his mind to see what he saw. Somehow, with ease, he could draw those images onto paper, bringing life to his imagination. Adam stopped drawing for several years, too many other distractions bidding for his young adult attention. But he's slowly returning to his interest in art again, even exploring other, more challenging media.

Which leads to my friend, Neil.

I met Neil, a well-known local artist, at a church we attended. I told Neil about Adam's talent and showed him some sketches. Impressed by his work at only fourteen years of age, Neil saw potential in Adam, enough that he suggested he mentor Adam to hone his skills. But then Neil suggested something unexpected—he asked me to come to art lessons with Adam. At first, I laughed at the suggestion, telling Neil, "I don't have an artistic bone in my body." I shrugged off the idea until Neil proffered that I may have more creative ability than I realized. Then Neil said something that got my attention.

He said, "Everyone is an artist. But not everyone knows it yet."

The following week, Adam and I sat in Neil's studio and our instruction began. Although we eventually worked with other media, we started with drawing. Adam was in his wheelhouse. Me? Well, I was in Neil's house, because that's where Neil's studio was, but that's as close to feeling at home as I could be.

We started by holding an object in our hand and Neil told us to draw what we saw. I grabbed a screwdriver because it was close by. Over the next few weekly sessions, Neil told us not to see a hand holding the object, but to look past the hand and the object to see the lines and shapes. Neil taught me not to see a finger or knuckle or screwdriver handle, but to see a series of lines and to draw the lines—to see shapes and draw them. Following Neil's instruction, I was shocked when my hand and the screwdriver disappeared and just lines and shapes emerged. It was as if my eyes shifted into another realm where I could see differently. As I drew what my new vision saw, I finished and on the page was a clear image of my hand holding a screwdriver.

Throughout this book I've written much about creating— creating a positive-focused, firm-grip life. But as you've read these pages, maybe you've had similar thoughts to mine when Neil asked me to come to art lessons:

I don't think that way.
I'm not creative.
So how could I ever create a new life?

You may be a lineal thinker, more interested in getting from point A to point B than what the scenery looks like along the way. You might look at an amazing painting on the wall of an art gallery and wonder how any human could create something so spectacular. Maybe you've heard a song that deeply moved you, and wished you could make beautiful music to stir others. I know these thoughts too. I've had a lifetime of them, wondering why I wasn't gifted with an artistic skill set.

It probably fell apart for us when we were little and someone told us to color between the lines, but our crayon wandered beyond, into what we saw in our imagination that no one else saw. We weren't thinking about how our coloring compared to the kid at the next desk. We were creating our masterpiece. But then a teacher said that our coloring wasn't good because we didn't stay in the lines. Everyone else was staying in the lines but us. We were told to be like everyone else and conform. So, we looked at the work of our friends and played the comparison game, comparing our projects to theirs, believing our work was inferior. Eventually, we concluded that our projects weren't any good, that we weren't creative people, that we're not artists. And that's how we've lived ever since.

Pablo Picasso said, "Every child is an artist. The problem is how to remain an artist once we grow up."

So, what if Neil was right? What if we're all artists, but just not yet aware of our creative genius? What if at the very core of our being is a soul that's designed to create? To dream? To bring things into existence that are beautiful and life-giving? What if we all had the DNA of a world class artist?

Created to Create

To explore my proposition further, we must return one more time to the Genesis poem where we find the first acts of God, acts of Divine creation.

"In the beginning God created the Heavens and the Earth."
Genesis 1:1 (NIV)

The first ten words of the Bible tell us of a Divine Being that creates something massive—the entire universe with the Earth placed in its midst. By anyone's measure, that's a monumental piece of work. And this creative act occurs within one day. Over the next several days, this Divine Being continues to create—light, dark, water, air, plants, and animals. After creating each of these, this Divine Being declared them as good.

Then came day six.

"Then God said, 'let us make mankind in our image, in our likeness, so that they may rule over the fish in the sea and the birds in the sky, over the livestock and all the wild animals, and over all the creatures that move along the ground.' So, God created mankind in his own image, in the image of God he created them; male and female he created them." Genesis 1:26-27 (NIV)

To be sure we wouldn't miss it, in those two short verses, we're told three times that God created mankind in his image. Mankind—that's us. You. Me. In the very image of God... this Divine Being... who made all things out of nothing and spoke them into existence. God put himself in humans like a spiritual DNA. And after God added humans to the mix, bearing the Imago Dei, God declared all that he had made as very good—it was no longer just good—it was very good! And just to solidify once and for all his intent that humans carry the image of the Divine, we're told....

"... the Lord God formed a man from the dust of the
ground and breathed into his nostrils the breath of life, and
man became a living being." Genesis 2:7 (NIV)

The very first breath a human ever breathed came from the lungs of God. God exhaled, and we inhaled. We are his creation. We bear his image. We have the DNA of the Divine. It would be difficult to argue there was any act more creative than that of the Divine bringing all things into existence. Our Creator is the greatest artist of all time. And he created us to continue to create, carrying out his image here on Earth.

I was created to create.

You were created to create.

When we create, we reflect the image of the Divine in us.

Why did I tell Neil I had no creative bones in my body

when in fact I have the breath of the Divine in my lungs?

A New Definition of Artist

Somewhere along our journey, we humans confused creating with art. We convinced ourselves that only artists create—that only those who paint beautiful pictures, or write inspiring poetry, or sing moving songs are artists. But what if the act of creating includes much more than making something to hang on your living room wall?

Creating simply means bringing into existence something that didn't previously exist.

My friend, Mark, builds custom homes. They are stunning. One includes a rounded wood barrel ceiling, another a free-floating staircase. Many have massive stone fireplaces and all include intricate details of a master craftsman. Handed a set of blueprints, an empty plot of ground, and a pile of materials, he creates stunning homes for people to live in and raise families. There was nothing—then there was a home.

Society calls Mark a contractor.

I call him one of the most talented artists I know.

Erin, another friend, teaches in our local high school. Erin is passionate about teaching, inspiring her students to excel not just in the classroom, but to become courageous people who pursue greatness in their lives while giving of themselves generously to others. For Erin, teaching is more than curriculum—teaching is shaping young minds to live a life beyond themselves that makes our world a better place. That process of shaping young minds is an act of creation—creating minds that think better at the end of the school year than on the first day of class.

Erin is an artist who creates beautiful minds.

I do a lot of contract negotiation for a particular client. Every time the negotiation succeeds, my client lands the deal. Every time my client lands the deal, they hire many people to fill the contract requirements. Each deal results in jobs being created, jobs that didn't exist when I woke up that morning. I often imagine someone phoning a significant other to share the news they've found a job, a job that now exists from the creative process of negotiating a contract. Someone once said negotiating is an art form. I think that person understood the creative process includes much more than paint on canvas.

Each of us *is* an artist
because we were created *by* an Artist
who designed us to create.

You have the spiritual DNA of the God who created the universe and everything in it. Maybe that comes as a surprise to you. Or maybe you can't think of anything you've created. But what about …

- Meals for your family.
- An arrangement of pictures on your wall.
- Peace in a child scared by a storm.
- A backyard garden and landscape.

- A project at work that helped better organize your company operations.
- Drawers full of clean laundry.
- A restored relationship.
- A stocked shelf at work, the items now ready for sale.
- A field full of crops that will feed thousands of people.
- Laughter and conversation with a dear friend.
- Lasting memories at the bedside of a dying loved one.
- The children in your home.

You see, anything that didn't exist, but came into existence because of your efforts, is a work you created. Today, you gave energy and effort to something and out of that work something now exists that didn't exist when you awoke this morning. Look at that list again. There is beauty in each of those creations and what each of them bring into your life and the lives of others around you. So, color outside the lines again. Embrace the artistic DNA you inherited from your Creator.

My friend Neil was right—
everyone is an artist, and that includes you.

Your Most Important Creation

So, it's true—you've already created many things during your lifetime. You created things today, and you will create things tomorrow. You will continue to create until your last breath. Some of your creations are more important than others. Who would argue that creating a human life is not more important than creating a ham sandwich? We'd all agree that creating healthy relationships is more significant than making a pot of coffee. But if there is only one thing you take away from this book, I pray it is this:

> The most important thing you will ever create
> is your life.

Every life is a work of art, created first by God. But after given the breath of God in our lungs, he hands the paintbrush to the creation to finish the work. That paint brush becomes the choices we make, each choice a stroke of the artist's brush, a picture slowly forming, a life evolving into something that didn't previously exist.

> Choice by choice,
> we create our lives.

I'm not suggesting God's work in us is complete when he handed us the brush. Rather, I'm confident he asks us to co-create our lives with him. He continues to hold the paint palette, suggesting colors even, but he lets us make the choices that result in the creation.

> And the life you create
> will be the most compelling work of art
> of your lifetime.

As we discussed in the second chapter of this book, there are parts of our lives over which we have no control, over which we have no choice. Those brush strokes simply happen—we were born with them, or they find their way into our lives. But even with the brush strokes we didn't get a choice to make, we still have the choice to decide how they will impact the final design. We can let the rough brush strokes ruin our lives through negative attitudes or we can choose to accept them and continue our work to co-create a masterpiece of incredible beauty, a life that reflects the image of the Divine within us, a firm-grip life.

Maybe you look at your life and see a lot of negative brush strokes through choices you've made, and you don't like the picture you've created. There's good news and great hope! Your masterpiece is still in process. Remember, as long as there's breath in you, you are still creating. All you have to do is pick up your paint brush and start making new brush strokes by making new choices. Choice by choice you can create a new life, a firm-grip life with a hopeful future. Your life is an organic piece of art, always being shaped, formed and sculpted—by you.

New Old Boards

Although I have no explanation for it, somehow cancer made me more aware of my creative nature. Maybe it's the way cancer helped change the lens through which I view life, to appreciate things I'd taken for granted previously. Maybe it's the way cancer slowed my pace, helped me restore healthy rhythms to my life. Likely, there was much at play in my life, much of which I may never realize. I only know that beauty became easier to recognize. I developed a new appreciation for art—not only traditional forms of art we see in an art gallery, but beautiful art in the form of great architecture, conversation with my tribe around a fire pit, the results achieved in helping people in my law practice, the relationships in my life—all great masterpieces that at one time didn't exist. Also, what grew in me was a desire to explore my creativity in new ways.

Several months after my diagnosis, I started pounding nails into old pieces of wood again. But this time it was different. It was more than just pounding nails—it was creating art. I selected pieces of reclaimed wood, old boards that presumably had already lived out their usefulness, discarded by someone who no longer saw value in them. They were full of imperfections—holes, stains, cracks, and blemishes. Using a small hammer that belonged to my grandfather, I pounded copper nails into them, creating patterns that made sense to me. I had no lines to stay within, but didn't care if I did. I created what I saw in my head, just like Adam drew what he saw. Some of my pieces of art now hang in my house and those of friends and family.

What's interesting about these pieces of old wood with copper nails is the way they reflect light. When viewed, and depending on where the viewer stands, the light either reflects off the copper nail heads, or the nail heads almost disappear. It's fun to watch people when they view the boards. As they stand in one location, the nails are almost invisible. Then they move and as they do, they'll eventually find a location from which the nail heads light up, as if someone flipped a switch and turned them on. When I created these pieces, I didn't realize the reflected light would impact how the pieces were seen. It just worked out that way.

The way the nails reflect light is like our lives. Most of the time, the view we have of our lives depends on where we choose to stand, the perspective we choose to take. When people view my art from a dark location, the art is boring; it makes no sense. But when they move to where the light reflects, everything changes. They smile, they laugh, they see it, and the art has meaning that elicits joyful emotion.

If you're standing in a place where your life looks dull and drab, uninteresting and negative, you have the choice to move. To choose a new location. To view your life from a different place, with a new perspective.

And when you choose to move to get a better view,
you begin the process of creating a new life—
a positive, hopeful, firm-grip life.

But you must create this life intentionally.
A firm-grip life doesn't just happen.
It's created by intent.

You only live the life
you choose to create.

Creating a positive-focused future starts by choosing to live with a positive focus in the present. Today. Here. Now. Don't wait for a future to arrive that looks no different than your present. The life you create today is a glimpse of the future you can live tomorrow. So, choose to create a positive present to shape a positive future. Author and theologian, Abraham Joshua Heschel said, "Above all, remember that the meaning of life is to live it as if it were a work of art."[1] He was right. Your life is a work of art and you co-create it alongside the greatest artist of all time.

And I suggest you listen to his color suggestions.
He's very good at it.

Conclusion:

Ruin or Rescue?

We have two lives; the one we learn with and the life after that.
—Bernard Malamud

There's an ancient parable about a woman distraught over the death of her young son. Desperate, she carried him through the village, looking for help to bring him back to life. Eventually the woman found a spiritual leader who told her he could help if she brought him four to five mustard seeds from a home within the village. The only condition was that the mustard seeds had to come from a home that had not suffered the death of a child, spouse, parent, sibling or friend. The woman began her frantic search for the mustard seeds, determined to find such a home. Many offered mustard seeds, but the woman could not find one home that had not experienced the death of a loved one. Finally understanding the teaching of the spiritual leader, the woman went home and buried her son, realizing that suffering finds everyone, that none are spared the pain of sorrow.

Life is hard, precarious, a risky proposition. It doesn't always go as planned. We all suffer, experience disappointment, pain, loss, fear, and grief. All these emotions are inevitable because we are human, created with the ability to feel our experiences, not just live them. But this book is about hope despite our struggle, joy despite our sorrow, and living with a firm-grip approach to life no matter what we face.

Any conversation about hope, joy, and living a positive, thriving life must begin with a conversation about suffering. There's something sacred about suffering because in God's economy, nothing is wasted, not even our suffering. It's through our darkest storms and deepest pain that we usually learn life's greatest lessons. The most positive, hope-filled people I've met have known great suffering. You see, it's not on the mountain tops where we grow most, but in the hard-fought valleys where darkness lurks.

Wildfires and Rescues

It seems every time I watch the news, a forest fire is raging somewhere, destroying thousands of acres of trees and vegetation, scattering wildlife and threatening homes and human life. Wildfires destroy everything in their path and leave an ashen heap of devastation in their smokey trails, nothing left.

But if we return to these sites' years later, we'd find trees and vegetation again, new growth, often including new species of life that didn't previously exist in that location. Wildlife returns, the ecosystem restores, and the area brims, abundant with new life. Given time, the ecosystem becomes stronger, healthier, and more sustainable.

The darkness that invades our lives is often like those forest fires. It blazes in and wreaks havoc, seemingly destroying everything in its path, leaving us with what seems like no life left, just a smoldering pile of ashes. We feel that all is lost, nothing remains to move forward with, to make a life from. I know that fire. But through that fire, our darkest times can clear the way for new, beautiful and abundant growth in our lives.

> Sometimes we have to lose the life we had
> to discover the life we are meant to live.
> Sometimes what appears to destroy us
> eventually rescues us.

Like a landscape destroyed in a wildfire takes decades to recover, it may take a long time before our rescue becomes evident after our lives are ravaged. Few would walk the scorched land after a wildfire and see hope for rescue from the devastation. It's easy to look at our lives after they've been wrecked and see no chance that a rescue is ever possible. The pain is just too intense, like a thousand-degree flame.

But there's always a rescue if we're willing to look for it. In fact, rescue is promised us by the prophet Isaiah who wrote, "Even to your old age and gray hairs I am he, I am he who will sustain you. I have made you and I will carry you; I will sustain you and I will rescue you." Isaiah 46:4 (NIV)

As I live more deeply into the firm-grip life, I've learned that through every dark storm or raging wildfire, there will be a rescue eventually, even if the rescue doesn't look like what I desired. Had God decided to end my life shortly after my diagnosis, that would have still been a rescue—a full, complete and total rescue. I've come to realize that people who die from cancer don't lose their battle, they're rescued *from* their battle.

> There are many ways rescue may show up in our lives.
> But it will always show up.

The firm-grip life believes in rescues, even when they're messy, complicated, and don't take the shape we'd hoped for. No matter what you've been through, like the forest after a wildfire, the firm-grip life believes that something will grow—no matter how long it may take— and it will be beautiful.

My Story—Your Story

I've shared my story in the pages of this book. I've told you of my darkest storms, greatest fears, and fiercest battles with a rare and incurable cancer. As that storm rolled in, it was horrific, like a wildfire raging through my life. But I survived. I'm still here. In fact, like the land after the fire, I now recognize the path this fire cleared in my life, allowing me to rise stronger, more grateful, hopeful, and wise. I now see that after the fire, there was a rescue—certainly a physical rescue, at least for now. But there was also rescue offered through the life markers of my life that led me to a new way to live, a better way of being human—the firm-grip way of life.

But unlike new vegetation that eventually regrows on its own, I had to choose to rise from my ashes, step out of my darkness into my rescue and into my future, choosing the attitude I would take with me. I saw two choices: bitter and negative or better and positive. My choice was clear—cancer didn't kill me, and I refuse to live my life as if it had. Creating a positive-focused, firm-grip life is about stepping out of our darkness, embracing all it can teach us and leaning into a future that we choose to create—a future full of hope. We may step out wobbly-kneed, uncertain, cautious, scared even, but firm-grip living always provides just enough courage to take that step, just enough light to see the path forward.

I hope as you've read these pages you've seen your story in my story. Felt your pain through my pain. Recognized your fears through my fears. Your darkness may feel like a fire that consumed even the soil, leaving no fertile ground from which anything could rise.

But you're still here, too. You survived. Maybe you're still surviving, one day at a time, but you're surviving. Everything that tried to destroy you, steal your life, rob your joy, kill you even—didn't! And you have today—this moment—*here.*

What are you going to do with this moment?

You can choose to see your darkness as nothing but disruption and pain that ruined your life, or you can choose to open yourself to what your darkness can teach you through a new way of seeing, thinking, and making choices—a rescue—a new way to thrive. You can stay in your old story, choosing despair and hopelessness or you can choose to step out of it and into a hopeful, new, firm-grip story, stronger, braver, wiser—better, not bitter.

The invitation of this book is to live a firm-grip life that gives you the courage and confidence to shift the way you think and make new choices that create a positive-focused present and hopeful future. It's possible, no matter what you've lived through. But it's a daily, often hourly, process of making choices that reorient your life to positive, hope-filled living; it's a lifelong process.

But it can start today.

Your life tells a story. The arch and trajectory of that story has a future, and it will carry a negative life narrative or a positive life narrative. That narrative will impact every person you encounter along the way. I hope this book reminded you how much control

you have over the narrative your life will carry forward, beginning...
right... now.

Putting Good in the World

The world desperately needs positive, hope-filled people more
than ever. At every intersection of life, we see people living on
autopilot, just trying to survive to the end of the day, overwhelmed
by the darkness in their lives, stressed over jobs, finances, and family
problems. Every day we're surrounded by people living unaware of
the good in their lives, with eyes that only see their darkness, trapped
in a negative mindset. There are people all around us, living in
despair, feeling hopeless, and desperate for rescue from negative lives.
The news, politics, and an increasingly divided society point to an
unsettling, negative future.

But we can create real change in the world around us.

To a great extent, this book has been about you. Changing your
life. Creating a better future for you. Living your firm-grip life. But it
has to start there because you can only take people where you have
been yourself. Living the firm-grip life isn't just about you. This isn't a
selfish act of just improving your life.

In the event of an emergency on an airplane, the oxygen masks
drop. The flight attendants always tell us to put our mask on first
before we help others with theirs. That's not a selfish act to assure
your survival. It's so you can remain healthy enough to assist others
with their mask so you can all survive. Maybe that's the ultimate and
greatest offering of this book—that you can offer hope, encourage

others, change lives and reshape the world around you simply by living your life with a positive, hope-filled, firm-grip attitude! Maybe you just need to put your mask on first.

Whether you realize it, you impact every room you walk into, every conversation you engage and every person you encounter. That impact will leave a positive or negative imprint. There is no neutral. When you choose to bring positive energy, your energy becomes contagious and lifts the people around you. Light always shines through the darkness. Hope always finds an eager ear and a positive attitude will always put good into the world.

There is always light somewhere.
The light just might be you!

First Steps to the Firm-Grip Life

If you don't know how to start living the firm-grip life, start here:

Start by choosing to see everything as a gift.
All of it.

Your tribe, even when relationships are hard.
Your job, even on the days you want to quit.
Your home, even if it's small.
Your money, even when it's not enough.

It's all a gift.
It's all a gift.
It's all a gift.

The beating heart in your chest.
The food on your table.
A friend who sits with you,
even when there's nothing to say.
A day of rest.
A slower paced life.
Clean water in your home.
A child on your lap.

It's all a gift.
It's all a gift.
It's all a gift.

The cherished memories of a loved one who died,
even though your heart aches.
The wrong done to you
because it gave you the opportunity to forgive.
The circumstance that caused fear
because it created the opportunity to trust.
The raging fire in your life
because it cleared the path for new growth.

The clash with cancer
because it showed me a better way of being human—
wiser,
kinder,
awake,
aware,
grateful.

It's all a gift.

It's all a gift.

It's all a gift.

Maybe this is what James meant when he wrote, "Consider it pure joy my brothers and sisters, whenever you face trials of many kinds, because you know the testing of your faith produces perseverance." James 1: 2-3 (NIV).

I'm convinced we can choose to live in such a way that we can embrace the trial (eventually) knowing that a rescue will rise from it that is life-giving and will reshape who we are and lead us from a scorched landscape to something more beautiful than we could ever imagine. That's the firm-grip life.

It's all a gift.

It's all a gift.

It's all a gift.

When you choose to view your life, what you have, the people who love you, the experiences you've lived, the joy, the triumphs, even the heartache, and the failures as a gift, you cultivate a place for gratitude to grow, gratitude that is the bass note of the firm-grip life.

Because it's impossible to live a negative life
when your heart is full of gratitude.

There's no getting this right, which means there's no getting it wrong. It will take time and intentional effort to create and live the firm-grip life. You'll still know pain, grief, anger, and every emotion that humans were created to experience. But in the firm-grip life, these emotions no longer control you. Some days will be easier than others. Some days will still suck. But it's not about the individual days. It's about creating a foundation in your life and posture of your soul from which you can see and engage the world around you with hope, no matter what is happening in your life.

It's all a gift!

You will choose, whether you realize it or not.
You will choose rescue or ruin--hope or despair.
The firm-grip life offers you rescue from ruin and despair.

But you have help.

Let me remind you one more time of your Creator's promise to you:

"Don't panic. I'm with you. There's no need to fear for I'm your God. I'll give you strength. I'll help you. I'll hold you steady, keep a firm grip on you."
Isaiah 41:10 (The Message)

As you create and live forward into the firm-grip life and a hope-filled future...

May you embrace gratitude as the bass note of your life.

May you be mindful of your life markers
and how you're engaging
the people in your life
and the world around you.

May you live
awake and aware
to the presence of the Divine
in you,
around you
and
in
every
single
moment.

May you realize
it's all a gift.

And may you cling to the unshakeable truth
that your life rests
in the firm grip of the Divine.

APPENDIX I

Places I Wrote this Book

My home in Northwest Indiana

Starbucks, Michigan City, IN

Starbucks, La Porte, IN

Lakeshore Coffee, Michigan City, IN

Peet's Coffee, Chicago, IL (North Side)

Starbucks, Mass Ave., Indianapolis, IN

Temple News Agency, La Porte, IN

Rocky Mountain Cafe, La Porte, IN

La Porte County Public Library, La Porte, IN

FLUID Coffee Bar, Valparaiso, IN

Starbucks, E. Flamingo Rd., Las Vegas, NV

Coat Check Coffee, Indianapolis, IN

Biggby Coffee, Michigan City, IN

Benny's Chop House, Chicago, IL

Starbucks, Omni Severin Hotel, Indianapolis, IN

Hyatt Regency Hotel, Indianapolis, IN

Calvin Fletcher's Coffee Company, Fountain Square, Indianapolis, IN

Square Cat Vinyl, Fountain Square, Indianapolis, IN

Infusco Coffee Roasters, Sawyer, MI

Goblin & The Grocer, Beverly Shores, IN

Stan's Donuts & Coffee, Chicago, IL

Starbucks, Cosmopolitan, Las Vegas, NV

Vanderbilt Country Club, Naples, FL

University Hospital, Indiana University Medical Center, Indianapolis, IN

FLUID Coffee Lounge and Roasting Laboratory, Michigan City, IN

Starbucks Reserve Roastery, Michigan Ave., Chicago, IL

A Whole World of Good, La Porte, IN

APPENDIX II

Scripture verses cited in this book are from the following Bible translations:

Unless otherwise indicated, all Scripture quotations are taken from the Holy Bible, New International Version ®, NIV® Copyright © 1973, 1978, 1984, 2011 by Biblica, Inc. ® Used by permission of Zondervan. All rights reserved worldwide. The "NIV" and "New International Version" are trademarks registered in the United States Patent and Trademark Office by Biblica, Inc.™

Scripture quotations marked MSG are taken from THE MESSAGE, copyright © 1993, 2002, 2018 by Eugene H. Peterson. Used by permission of NavPress. All rights reserved. Represented by Tyndale House Publishers, Inc.

Scripture quotations marked (ESV) are taken from the ESV® Bible (The Holy Bible, English Standard Version®), copyright © 2001 by Crossway, a publishing ministry of Good News Publishers. Used by permission. All rights reserved.

Scripture quotations marked (NLT) are taken from the Holy Bible, New Living Translation, copyright © 1996, 2004, 2015 by Tyndale House Foundation. Used by permission of Tyndale House Publishers, a Division of Tyndale House Ministries, Carol Stream, Illinois 60188. All rights reserved.

Scripture quotations marked (KJV) are taken from the KING JAMES VERSION (KJV): KING JAMES VERSION, public domain.

ACKNOWLEDGMENTS

Few things created, this book included, are the result of a single person's efforts. The creative process is itself the culmination and expression of the actions and influences of those who helped shape the creator. This book, the ideas in its pages, the message I hope it offers, are the result of many people who spoke wisdom and truth into my life over many decades. Others literally took actions that saved my life, or helped share my story, or offered their expertise, or simply loved me well. This book would not be possible without each of you.

My profound gratitude goes to…

Melissa Wuske for your brilliant editing expertise, guidance, patience, and most of all, encouragement through each draft—and the next one, and the next one, and the next one. You saw my story between the lines and helped bring it to these pages.

The team at Gatekeeper Press, including Sarah Duckworth, Rob Price, Haroula Kontorousi, Dawn Greer, Tia Mele, and Davor Dramikanin. Your tireless efforts helped put the message of this book into the world.

Jane Friedman, author, teacher, and publishing-world guru, for taking this first-time author under your wing and sharing your wisdom, experience, and advice that kept me from crashing and burning. You laid out the path; I simply followed it.

Lisa Haneberg, multi-book author, friend, and fellow MTC warrior. In the middle of your journey, one far more difficult than writing a book, you were there, answering each call, replying to every email, fielding all my questions, but mostly, telling me each time that I could do this.

Tom Plantz for your meaningful contribution to the book cover design.

My medical team, particularly Dr. Avinash Mantravadi, Dr. Matthew Provenzano and Dr. Jamie Stickley. I'm here on the sunny side of this Earth and could write this book because you all did your jobs—really, really well. I'm telling you once again that each of you saved my life, and I will never stop thanking you.

Miki Young for your friendship and spending a grueling day sitting in the hospital with Jane through my surgery, waiting for me to wake up.

Julie West for the privilege of sharing your story and your journey of transforming the tragic loss of Jake into a mission to save the lives of young adults. Julie, you are a beautiful example of waking up each day and choosing hope over despair and living the firm-grip life. You are amazing!

Chuck Smith and Dave Lewis. You both walked through the dark long before me, leaving a trail of light to help me find my way. In some of my darkest times, it was only the light you shared that helped me take my next step.

Gerry and Roxy Wiley for your roles in my life as life coaches, spiritual mentors, and friends. Gerry, you've always reminded me to look for what's true. Roxy, you gave me the packet of cards that led me to the firm-grip life. You've both modeled the firm-grip life for decades. Now I know what to call it.

My parents, Bill Sr. and Jan, for raising me on a path that led to my firm-grip life. I love and miss you both.

My tribe—you know who you are.

My fellow MTC Warriors in our corner of the internet who talked me off the ledge more times than I can count in the early days of my cancer journey. You are amongst the most courageous people I've ever known, and each of you inspire me daily.

George Labonte for your never-ending inspiration. You simply amaze me brother!

Rod Bensz for... oh my, where do I start?
-for going to Haiti with me.
-for the joy of being godfather to your children.
-for being the best example of authenticity I've witnessed.
-for your selflessness and kindness.
-for taking Jane and me on a boat across Lake Michigan to a Cold Play concert (yes, it meant that much to me, especially that year).
-for the "Undetectable T-Shirt."
-for always being there—always.

Mark and Lesa Hill for… well, there's nothing I can write here that touches the depth of my gratitude for the gift of you in my life. For more than four decades, our lives have been intertwined—strands in a rope, making each other stronger. There are few things we've lived that weren't experienced together. You've supported me (and Jane) through it all—the good, the bad, and the really hard stuff, especially my darkest days written about in these pages. Whatever eternity looks like, I'm confident of one thing—you'll be there by my side, and I by yours.

Erik and Adam for making me so proud to be your father. I've learned from each of you how to better live my life as you are constant reminders of what matters. My greatest hope for you is that you will embrace and live the firm-grip life, confident you are held firmly in the hand of the Divine.

My wife Jane Nelson. Somehow, I'm supposed to figure out how to thank you in a few lines for your love, support, encouragement, and contribution to this book and my life.

Really?

That's somehow possible?

All I know is just about everything I write about in this book isn't possible without you. This journey with cancer, and all it taught me about living, is just as much your story as mine; it's our journey—it's our life. And like everything else we've experienced, we took each step together, as we will continue to do until our last day. So, until that day comes, I am here for you as you are for me, and we will keep taking steps into whatever is next.

Because that's what we do.

Together.

Always.

END NOTES

Chapter 01: Our Thoughts Matter

1. Lillian Eichler Watson, Light from Many Lamps, (New York: Simon and Schuster, 1951), pp.169-174.
2. Arthur L. Young, Attitude and Altitude, (New Outlook: Volume 8, Number 11, November, 1955), p.42.

Chapter 03: Every Day Has its Night

1. Louie Giglio, The Comeback, (Nashville, TN: W. Publishing Group, an imprint of Thomas Nelson, Inc., 2015), p.99.

Chapter 05: A Better Way of Being Human

1. Erwin Raphael McManus, Uprising, (Nashville, TN: Thomas Nelson, Inc., 2003), p.9.
2. The Rocketboys, "Like Ice in Water," track 4 on 20,000 Ghosts, Independently Recorded, 2009, The Rocketboys LLC, compact disc.
3. Ibid.

Chapter 09: Asking the Wrong Questions

1. Mark Synnott, The Impossible Climb, (New York, New York: Dutton, an imprint of Penguin Random House LLC, 2018), p.239.
2. Ibid.
3. Elizabeth Gilbert, *Big Magic*, (New York, New York: Riverhead Books, an imprint of Penguin Random House LLC, 2015), p.26.

Chapter 13: When Less is More

1. Mary MacVean, "For Many People, Gathering Possessions is Just the Stuff of Life." Los Angeles Times, March 21, 2014, https://latimes.com/health/la-xpm-2014-mar-21-la-he-keeping-stuff-20140322-story.html (accessed Nov. 23, 2018).

Chapter 21: Here, Not There

1. Richard Rohr, *Everything Belongs*, (New York, New York: The Crossroad Publishing Company, 1999, 2003), p.29.

Chapter 22: Old Boards and Copper Nails

1. Abraham Joshua Heschel, "Carl Stern's Interview with Dr. Heschel," in Moral Grandeur and Spiritual Audacity, (New York, New York: Noonday Press, 1996), p.412.

CONNECT WITH THE AUTHOR

Bill would love to hear from his readers. Email him at
bill@billnelsonauthor.com.

Or visit his website at
www.billnelsonauthor.com
for more opportunities to connect.

You can also follow him on social media—

Facebook: www.facebook.com/billnelsonauthor or
@billnelsonauthor

Twitter: @_billnelson

Instagram: @_billnelson_

Send Bill an email if you're interested in scheduling him
to speak at events, conferences, seminars, or even small
gatherings. He'd love to engage with your group, team, or
organization.